Mindfulness & the ADHD Parent:

Cultivating Calm and Building Connection

A Workbook

Recommended for: 5-12 years of age

NICOLE ANDREOLI, PHD

Dedication

To Chris and Domenica, who taught me the true meaning of love, collaboration, kindness, compassion and patience.

With gratitude, to my patients: thank you for allowing me to be a part of your path towards healing and growth. I have learned so much from our time working together. You have taught me about courage, resilience, and the incredible power of the human spirit. Thank you for your stories and for allowing me to bear witness to your struggles and triumphs. I am constantly inspired by your strength and willingness to confront the challenges that life presents.

As a psychologist, it is my job to help guide you towards greater self-awareness and self-acceptance, but it is you who have done the hard work of facing fears, dealing with the uncomfortable and taking steps towards your goals. I am grateful to have been a part of that process, and for the knowledge and experience I have gained along the way.

May this book serve as a small token of my appreciation and a testament to the incredible impact you have had on my professional journey.

Contents

Dedication iii

Introduction 1

Part 1: Mindfully Parenting A Child With ADHD 5

Introduction 5

Chapter 1: Understanding Your Child's Experience with ADHD...7

Case Study 8

The Impact of ADHD on Executive Function Skills 15

Key Takeaways 23

Chapter 2: The Foundation of Mindful Parenting for ADHD 25

Case Study 27

What Is Mindful Parenting? 27

Key Takeaways 46

Part II: Transforming Yourself Into A Mindful Parent 47

Chapter 3: Make Your Needs a Priority 48

Introduction 48

Case Study 50

Key Takeaways 74

Chapter 4 Reacting Calmly to Chaos as a Parent 76

Introduction.. 76

Case Study 77

Key Takeaways.. 99

Chapter 5: Parenting Positively 100

Case Study 101

Key Takeaways 118

Chapter 6: Active Listening 119

Case Study 120

Key Takeaways... 138

PART III: Practicing Mindfulness Skills for ADHD with Your Child
....139

Chapter 7: Developing Shared Goals and Expectations 139

Introduction... 139

Case Study 140

Key Takeaways.. 155

Chapter 8: Staying Calm, Focused, And In Control 157

Case Study 158

Key Takeaways... 170

Chapter 9: Improving Executive Functioning Skills 171

Introduction... 171

Case Study 171

Key Takeaways 190

Chapter 10: Creating Healthy Family Routines........................191

Introduction... 191

Case Study 192

Key Takeaways 204

Chapter 11: Building On What's Working 205

Introduction... 205

Case Study 206

Key Takeaways 217

Back Matter..219

A Final Note.. 219

Resources 221

References...222

About The Author 230

Introduction

Welcome! Since you are reading this book, you are likely already in the throes of parenting a child with challenging behaviors. This type of parenting is both physically and emotionally exhausting, whether or not your child meets criteria for Attention Deficit Hyperactivity Disorder (ADHD).

I want to let you in on a secret: you are not alone. I've counseled many families in your shoes. Secondly – and this is almost more important – ADHD extends far beyond a child's inability to maintain attention or control the energy in their body. It disrupts family dynamics, creates chaos and causes arguments, and lurks behind eating habits and bedtime routines. It shows up at inconvenient, often embarrassing times, such as church, playdates and restaurants. It may cause strife between you and your child, you and your spouse, and between your child and their siblings, peers and teachers. It is the uninvited guest whose presence you dreadfully anticipate and loathe.

While you love your child – after all, that is why you are here - the dichotomy of emotions you feel towards your child may also create feelings of shame and guilt for you. Let me assure you, it is *absolutely OK* to admit that as much as you love your child, there are aspects of them you find challenging and difficult. These feelings can coexist, and the fact that they coexist does not make you a bad parent. Likewise, they certainly do not mean you love your child any less. These feelings make you human, and they make you real. This acknowledgment is your first mindfulness lesson. Parenting is complex. Love is complex. There are layers to our relationships and the reality is that they may not all be positive.

Acknowledgements, such as this one, is a cornerstone of mindfulness theory. To me, it is not only an important one, but a significant first step in a mindfulness journey. In my work as a psychologist, I stress the importance of acknowledging the reality of our situation, and of our thoughts and emotions. If can be freeing to stop pretending, or to stop avoiding the truth. I have seen many times the positive impact *acknowledgment* plays in mental health.

My journey evaluating and treating children began as a doctoral student. My experience since then includes working in a school developing programs to help navigate the systems and supports necessary to aid learning for children with behavioral and emotional disorders. In my private practice, I conduct evaluations to identify and diagnose ADHD (among other disorders). Once evaluated, I create treatment plans and make recommendations that will help parent and child work through symptomatic difficulties. This book is a culmination of my experience working with children with emotional and behavioral challenges. The more I worked, the more I saw the positive impact that mindfulness theory has had on both parents and children.

While a workbook is a great way to work through the challenges of parenting a child with ADHD, any debilitating feelings of depression or anxiety should be addressed by a medical professional. While this workbook is a great addition to your toolbox, it is not a replacement for mental health treatment. There is no shame in seeking help or treatment.

The mindfulness journey is an exciting one, and I am honored to embark on it with you. The pages of this book will hopefully lead you to a strong mindfulness practice, and positive outcomes such as improved parent-child communication, and parenting satisfaction, as well as decreased symptoms of anxiety, depression, aggression and hyperactivity.

How to Use this Book

This book is divided into three parents.

Part I, "Mindfully Parenting a Child with ADHD," contains foundational information about parenting children with ADHD and how to practice mindfulness as a parent. Part II, Transforming Yourself into a Mindful Parent, contains workbook elements designed for parents to practice mindfulness on their own. Part III, Practicing Mindfulness Skills for ADHD with your Child, includes workbook elements that parents can do collaboratively with their children to mindfully address their ADHD symptoms.

Parts II and III contain hands on exercises designed to help you learn, practice and apply mindfulness skills. These skills are presented in the form of case studies, prompts, practices and exercises. These two parts also begin with an affirmation, which you can repeat to yourself or write on a note to post around your space to uplift and encourage you to continue your practice.

While this workbook is designed for parents of children ages 5 to 12, where appropriate, I will provide more specific advice tailored to younger or older children. Note that mindfulness practices are appropriate for individuals across the lifespan, so feel free to make any appropriate modifications that you feel are necessary.

Part 1:
Mindfully Parenting A Child With ADHD

Introduction

Congratulations on taking the first step towards a healthier, calmer way of parenting your child with ADHD. You are likely feeling overwhelmed, stressed, frustrated, and tired. As I've mentioned before, parents of children with ADHD struggle not only with managing their children, but also with higher levels of anxiety and depression. This can ultimately translate into higher levels of family and marital discord as compared to other families. Anyone can benefit from adopting strategies rooted in mindfulness theory, but parents of children who have ADHD will find mindfulness practices particularly valuable.

This workbook highlights the key aspects of a transformative mindfulness practice. The tools in this book encourage and explore how to take care of yourself through mindfulness and compassion, and then apply these practices to navigate the tumultuous ride that is parenting.

Part I of this book lays the foundation for understanding what ADHD is (and is not). We also touch on components of mindful parenting, and how mindfulness can help lead to better, calmer outcomes for both you and your child.

Read the chapters of this book in order, but revisit topics as needed to refresh or for mastery. I like to remind the patients that I work with that not every technique will work every day. On some days, one strategy may be more effective than others. There is no magic intervention that guarantees perfect results every time. It's better to build a therapeutic toolbox of strategies that you practice, and that you know work for you. Keep note of the techniques that you learn, note how they make you feel, and keep practicing! These techniques will become a wonderful resource for both you and your child.

Chapter 1:

Understanding Your Child's Experience with ADHD

If you have read this far, then you are already familiar with the struggle that is parenting a child with ADHD. You understand how hard it is to *parent,* but I bet you struggle to understand why your child behaves the way they do and why they can't seem to change or improve their behavior. This chapter offers a brief overview of what ADHD is, the changes it causes in the brain, and how that affects your child's behavior. I also include a section on what the ADHD experience is like from your child's perspective, as well as the influence that ADHD has on everything from the larger family system, to school and friendships.

There is hope for your child with ADHD. As will be discussed, there are strengths associated with the diagnosis. There is also help and support that both you and the school can provide, so that you can help your child reach their potential and attain the best possible outcomes.

My hope is that the information here provides parents a better understanding of ADHD and gives you the tools necessary to respond to your child's behavior with a compassionate, focused and mindful approach.

Case Study

Risa is 8 years old with a diagnosis of ADHD, hyperactive-impulsive subtype. In most classes, Risa struggles to stay in her seat and not talk to her neighbor. Risa admits to her parents that she "forgets" to stay quiet, and always promises to try harder.

Risa's favorite subject is history, but she often gets into trouble while her teacher, Mr. Matthews, is teaching. This is because she frequently answers questions aloud without raising her hand. Mr. Matthews has asked Risa numerous times to give the other students a chance to answer questions. Rita tried to comply, and for a while, she would blurt out answers but then remember that she wasn't supposed to do that and would quickly yell, "I forgot!" She was catching her impulsivity seconds too late to change the behavior.

Risa and her parents enrolled in a mindfulness program to help Risa learn to better regulate her impulsivity. Risa learned basic mindfulness practices, such as deep breathing and how to take a mindful pause, as well as a pause button meditation. Before speaking, she imagines pressing an imaginary button underneath her desk, while taking slow, deep breaths. This helps her to pause for a second and collect her thoughts before impulsively answering.

Risa has been using this trick for a few weeks now. Mr. Matthews notices how hard Risa is working, and the positive affect it is having on her impulsivity. Every time Mr. Matthews sees Risa trying to use her pause button meditation, he praises her effort. This validation has helped Risa feel especially proud and motivates her to keep practicing.

What It's Like to Have ADHD as a Child

ADHD is considered to be the most common neurodevelopmental disorder. Symptoms typically appear in childhood, and mainly center around *inattention,* which can present as a child being forgetful, having trouble focusing, or paying attention. Another component is *hyperactivity* and *impulsivity,* which can look like not waiting for their turn to speak (like Risa in the case study), or difficulty staying seated or waiting their turn.

ADHD symptoms usually begin to emerge by ages 3-4 and are formally diagnosed at around 5 years of age, right around when the behaviors become impactful in an academic setting. Symptoms can range from *mild* impairment to *severe.* Children with mild impairment have enough symptoms to meet criteria for a diagnosis, but there is only a minor influence in school or behavioral functioning. Severe impairment means that the child possesses a high number of symptoms, or symptoms create a marked impairment in their academic or behavioral functioning.

Within the spectrum of mild to severe ADHD, there are three subtypes of ADHD:

- Predominately Inattentive Type, which is characterized by behaviors such as being easily distracted, difficulty focusing and poor organizational skills.
- Predominately Hyperactive / Impulsive Type, which is characterized by being talkative and fidgety, and difficulty staying on task.
- Combined Type (Symptoms of both Inattention and Hyperactive / Impulsive), which is characterized by both inattentive and hyperactive / impulsive behaviors.

Your child may possess a unique cluster of symptoms. The symptoms can change over time, so they way that ADHD presents in your child today is likely to look different as they get older.

Inattention

An inattentive child may daydream, show poor effort in schoolwork, need reminders to do things, not follow directions, struggle with organization, and have poor follow-through. Older kids have trouble setting and maintaining priorities, attaining goals, and keeping track of deadlines.

Signs of inattention include:

- Difficulty sustaining attention
- Careless mistakes
- Difficulty organizing

10

- Struggling with directions
- Losing things
- Easily distracted
- Forgetfulness

It is important to remember that these symptoms are outside of the child's control. They cannot simply be told to *"apply yourself"* or *"just focus"*- two commands I hear often from the parents of my patients – in order to be successful. As we will discuss, there are neurological differences in an ADHD brain, that translates to differences in executive function related skills and abilities. Simply put, the child's brain will not let them *just focus,* or *try harder.* That's where skills such as mindfulness come in.

An interesting fact about the inattentive subtype: it is more prevalent in females. It also often goes missed and undiagnosed, specifically in children who show more of the internalized behaviors, such as daydreaming and forgetfulness, but manage to attain good grades.

Hyperactivity and Impulsiveness

Children that meet this criterion may jump or roughhouse when it's time to play quietly. They rush instead of taking their time, seem unable to sit still, and interrupt or blurt out a lot. A child with hyperactivity and impulsiveness will talk without thinking. They also have trouble taking turns, waiting or sharing. As these kids get older, the hyperactivity tends to decline. However, in teen years, the impulsivity may translate into risk taking behavior, such as lying, stealing, and substance use.

Signs of hyperactivity / impulsiveness include:

- Fidgets when seated
- Struggles to stay seated
- Overly talkative
- Difficulty waiting turn
- Interrupts / intrudes on conversations and activities of others
- Appears to be driven by a "motor," always on the go

It is important to note that regardless of symptom presentation, emotional challenges for these children typically go together. Imagine constantly being in trouble by your parents and teachers for behaviors that you cannot control, such as not being able to remain seated, forgetting to do something, or losing your notebook. Children with ADHD become acutely aware that they are different from their peers. They may also realize how hard they are trying to control or improve the problematic behavior and start to internalize that failure. For these reasons, these children are at higher risks for low self-esteem and anxiety disorders, with the severity of ADHD symptoms predicting the severity of the comorbid conditions. These emotional symptoms are intensified when another disorder, such as a learning disability, is coexisting. Some researchers estimate that 87 percent of children with any type of ADHD may have another disorder, and 67 percent may have at least two others.

How ADHD Affects the Whole Family

A child's diagnosis of ADHD can have unexpected consequences on the entire family. Parents are at an increased likelihood of experiencing negative ramifications, since managing ADHD symptoms and behaviors can be difficult and overwhelming. Feelings of frustration and anxiety, and perhaps sadness, guilt or shame are the most common among parents whose child is diagnosed with ADHD. According to the Journal of Consulting and Clinical Psychology, marital conflict, as well as divorce rates, is higher in families where children have ADHD.

Researchers at Oregon Health Science University found that the family environment tends to be less organized and higher in conflict. Siblings have historically described family life as chaotic, conflictual, and exhausting. According to researchers at Old Dominion University, they tend to be the victims of their siblings' disruptive behaviors, including physical and verbal aggression, hyperactivity, and emotional and social immaturity.

Siblings may feel jealousy, anger, or resentment of the amount of parental attention the child with ADHD receives. They may act out to attract attention from their parents. Some children feel increased pressure to be "good," and not further stress parents. Siblings may feel embarrassed or shameful if their sibling is acting out in public. These negative emotions may result in conflict amongst siblings, as well as the siblings developing their own emotional or behavioral difficulties.

While this may sound bleak, rest assured that there are solutions that can help. Therapy, behavior management programs and medications are amongst the many options for the child with ADHD. Mindfulness practices for parents and siblings, such as

APPRECIATING THE STRENGTHS OF ADHD

In this book we will spend a fair amount of time discussing the challenges of ADHD. However, there is a positive side to ADHD as well. Many people report possessing *positive* attributes that are thought to compensate for the impairments related to ADHD. For example, in a large study of individuals diagnosed with ADHD, the journal of attention deficit and hyperactivity disorders found that many individuals report similar personal strengths, or "superpowers." Some of these positive traits include an abundance of:

1. Mental activity, such as heightened creativity as well as the ability to hyper focus
2. Courage, being able to confront fears and tolerate uncertainty
3. Energy, including an appreciation of the physical, spiritual, and psychological realms
4. Social behavior, including humor, recognition of feelings, social intelligence, and self-acceptance
5. Resiliency, including protective strengths that enable them to flourish despite adverse conditions
6. Appreciation of music and art

Other research adds traits such as optimism, adventurousness, curiosity and being able to live in the moment as strengths related to ADHD. It is important that the child's support network - parents, teachers, coaches, tutors, and therapists – focus on, praise, and harness these strengths so that they can help build self-esteem, as well as help the child succeed.

meditation and acceptance, are some of the tools that will be discussed in Parts II and III of this book.

The Impact of ADHD on Executive Function Skills

Executive function refers to the mental skills that permit problem-solving behavior that is geared towards attaining a goal. This includes being able to set goals, organize a plan to achieve the goal, adjust or shift the plan as needed and ultimately follow through to goal completion.

Executive function impairments may look different in each child, but generally, children with ADHD have difficulty with these tasks at home, in school, and in relationships. These individuals struggle with organization and self-regulation in ways that hinder goal-directed behavior.

Executive function consists of seven types of self-regulation:

- *Self-Awareness*, or self-directed attention
- *Self-Restraint*, or the ability to inhibit yourself
- *Non-Verbal Working Memory*, the ability to hold written things in mind
- *Verbal Working Memory*, the ability to hold spoken language in mind
- *Emotional*, the ability to use words and images along with self-awareness to alter how you feel about things

- *Self-Motivation*, the ability to motivate yourself to do things when no outside consequences exist
- *Planning and Problem Solving*, the ability to find new approaches and solutions

Dr Robert Brown, a psychiatrist who created psychological tools to measure executive dysfunction, describes six areas of executive functions that tend to be impaired in individuals with ADHD: activation, focus, effort, emotion, memory, and action.

Activation: organizing tasks and materials, estimating time, getting started

Children with this type of impairment tend to have difficulty organizing tasks and materials. They may struggle with estimating time and prioritizing their tasks. They often have trouble getting started on their work.

In children, this can look like forgetfulness or carelessness. Parents and teachers may have to constantly remind the child to stay on track, help them with keeping their tasks and materials organized, and help them to prioritize their tasks.

Focus: finding, sustaining, and shifting attention as needed

These children tend to lose focus when trying to listen or plan and tend to be easily distracted. They also forget what was read and may need to re-read.

In younger children, this may look like they are disinterested in what is going on. Parents and teachers may need to continually redirect, or bring their focus back to the task at hand.

Effort: regulating alertness, sustaining motivation and processing speed

Children with impairment in this area may have difficulty in regulating their sleep and their alertness. They may lose interest in tasks or long projects quickly and have difficulty completing tasks on time.

Emotion: managing frustration and modulating feelings

These children struggle managing and regulating emotions. They may experience intense frustration, irritation, hurt, and worry, and have a hard time navigating those feelings.

Memory: using working memory and accessing recall

Children with impairment in this category may have difficulty attending to multiple tasks at a single time. They have difficulty "remembering to remember" things and have trouble with recall.

Action: monitoring and regulating physical activity

This type of impairment makes it difficult for children to slow or speed themselves up, as needed for tasks. They may also have difficulty monitoring and modifying their actions to fit certain situations.

In children, this can look like running around in a classroom when all the other children are sitting.

If you suspect that your child may be showing symptoms of ADHD, it is important that they receive a comprehension evaluation. There are several benefits to psychological or neuropsychological testing. An assessment will help identify the root cause of your child's symptoms of hyperactivity and inattentiveness, as ADHD is only one possible explanation. An evaluation may show if there are other reasons contributing to or exacerbating behaviors, such as anxiety or sadness. It will also identify your child's strengths and weaknesses and help determine the best course of treatment for their unique presentation.

The components of the evaluation may vary depending on each child's specific symptoms, but tests typically examine all areas of functioning, including:

Getting an Evaluation and Diagnosis for Your Child

- Interviewing the parent and child (*if age appropriate*)
- Reviewing medical history and school records
- Child, parent and teacher completed behavior rating scales
- Intelligence testing
- Academic achievement testing / learning disability screening
- Neuropsychological assessment
- Emotional assessment
- Home or school observations
- Vision and / or hearing screening

An ADHD evaluation can be a long and overwhelming process that may require several hours of testing spread out over multiple days. Try to be patient and remember that there are a significant number of benefits to this type of psychological testing, including:

- Increased accuracy of diagnosis

- Increased understanding of the unique ways your child functions, cognitively, emotionally, behaviorally and personality-wise
- A clearer understanding of problematic behaviors
- Insight into functional areas that need additional support, and what the best support might be
- Insight into areas of strength as well

An assessment will provide insight into how your child thinks and processes information, how they learn, how they perform emotionally, and how exactly they are struggling. All this knowledge can then be used to help determine what the most effective intervention and treatment options are for your child.

How to Support Your Child with ADHD

Children with ADHD are in a difficult situation. They are at the center of a network of chaos and disorganization stemming from their behavioral and / or academic struggles. Because of these struggles, there may be additional issues at school with teachers or staff. Peer relationships may begin to suffer. Home life may become challenging, as the strain of having a child in the house with ADHD can impact siblings and parents. Self-esteem may then start to decline, and issues with anxiety and sadness may begin to creep in. With this spider web of negativity quickly spinning, how can parents best support their child?

Early intervention is vital in giving children with ADHD the best prognosis, as it hopefully stops symptoms from further decline. It is important to get supports, processes and routines in place as quickly as possible. Here are some specific tips on how to support your child at home and at school.

- **At Home.** While later parts of this book will discuss interventions to support your child, here are a few additional points:
- **Support Yourself.** Ensure that *you* are well supported. Are your own emotions managed? Are you engaging in self-care? Therapy can keep you accountable. Parent and / or family therapy is a good resource for behavior management skills and working through any negativity that arises.
- **Support Your Child.** Parenting in general is hard, and regardless of if your child has an ADHD diagnosis or not there will be hard times. Your relationship with your child matters most, and for these reasons, it is imperative that you do these 3 things often:
  - Tell your child you love and support them, period.
  - Apologize when you are in the wrong.
  - Identify and celebrate your child's strengths.
- **At School.** The best way to support your child at school is to become their number one advocate. Learn as much as you can about ADHD, and specifically how it presents in your child. Psychological testing can help with this, as well as give you clear direction on what

supports your child needs to be successful. Educate yourself on the rules and guidelines for your school district and ensure that your child receives the necessary academic or behavioral supports. Depending on your child's needs, these accommodations may include extended time on tests, small class sizes, tutoring, opportunities for movement or minibreaks, or even an Individualized Educational Plan (IEP) or Section-504. Collaborate and communicate with all teachers and tutors so that everyone is working towards common goals.

How Your Support Benefits Your Child

It's important to highlight the far-reaching benefits of strong parental support. *Regardless of income level or background, the greatest predictor of academic success, including better grades and better attendance, is parental involvement.* Children of supportive parents tend to have lower rates of substance abuse and risk-taking behavior, better social skills, increased self-esteem, and higher aspirations. There are mental health benefits as well, such as being at a decreased risk for developing depression. In children already struggling, parental support is going to be even more critical.

Despite your best intentions, parenting is hard! What can you do in a challenging moment to remember to keep calm, so that you can be a supportive parent? You need a mantra. Mantras are simple words or phrases that you repeat to yourself when you need to remain calm. Research shows that paired with deep breathing, mantras can help quiet the mind and calm the body.

Your mantra can be any word or phrase that is meaningful to you. In this instance, helpful mantras might be:

Choose kindness

I will pause before I react

It's just a tough moment

Connect before I correct

I am exhaling calmness.

When triggered in a challenging parenting moment, stop what you are doing and count to 10.

Take a slow, deep inhale. Pause. Exhale.

Repeat this breathing cadence as you say your mantra.

Repeat this exercise until you feel your body reach a state of calm. At that point, you can thoughtfully respond to your child.

Key Takeaways

This chapter introduced the ADHD brain and highlighted how it can affect the whole family since managing related symptoms and behaviors can be difficult and overwhelming. This underscores the importance of getting your child evaluated to determine if your child does have ADHD, if there are other diagnoses contributing to symptoms, your child's strengths and weaknesses, and the best course of treatment for your child.

Key Takeaways:

- There are 3 subtypes of ADHD: predominately inattentive, predominately hyperactive / impulsive, and combined type.
- Early intervention is vital.
- In addition to weaknesses, there are also strengths or "superpowers" associated with ADHD.
- Supporting your child starts with parental self-care.
- Be your child's advocate to ensure they get the supports they need.
- Find a mantra to use in challenging parenting moments.

Chapter 2:
The Foundation of
Mindful Parenting for ADHD

"The secret of health for both mind and body is not to mourn for the past, not to worry about the future, or not to anticipate troubles, but to live in the present moment wisely and earnestly."

- Buddha

Mindfulness theory comes from Buddhism and focuses on living in the present moment with less judgment and more acceptance. Throughout this workbook, we will talk about ways to incorporate the practice of mindfulness into your daily life. Research has found mindfulness leads to positive changes in almost every area of mental health: including decreased ruminating thoughts, stress, and sleep disturbances, as well as improvements in memory, emotional reactivity, and overall mood.

Mindfulness is a practice that involves focusing on the present moment without judgment. It involves consciously paying attention to one's thoughts, feelings, and body sensations with a non-judgmental attitude. This practice can be used to reduce stress, increase self-awareness, and promote emotional regulation. Mindfulness can be incorporated into daily life through activities such as meditation, mindful eating, mindful walking, and body scans. It can also be applied to everyday activities like being mindful of how you talk to yourself, being aware of your thoughts and feelings, and noticing how you react to different situations. Practicing mindfulness can help to reduce rumination and promote more positive outlooks. It can also help to improve sleep and decrease stress levels. As you practice mindfulness, you will become more aware of how your mind works and how to better manage your thoughts and emotions.

A mindful parenting style involves being less reactive to our children's behaviors and instead responding thoughtfully. This type of intentional reaction is about being present and pausing so that you can respond instead of reacting. Improving mindful parenting involves:

- Reflecting on previous, challenging exchanges with our children and looking for triggers and patterns in our reactions;
- Implementing techniques to help stay calm and composed when parenting is difficult;
- Working through our biases and/ or experiences;
- Implementing mindfulness strategies to help ensure better responses and a deeper understanding of children's behavior

This chapter opens with a discussion of what mindfulness is. The chapter will then introduce specific ways to practice and apply skills that will help you parent more mindfully.

26

Case Study

Marta is the mother of 7-year-old Jonah and 4-year-old Tabitha. Jonah was diagnosed with ADHD – Combined Type last year. While many of his behaviors are well-managed, Jonah often struggles with his sister. They argue over toys, have difficulty sharing, and Jonah often responds aggressively. Marta, Jonah, and Tabitha were stuck in the house on a rainy Saturday afternoon when Jonah and Tabitha began arguing over some blocks. Toys were thrown, and a juice box was spilled. Jonah was yelling, and Tabitha began crying. Before her mindfulness training, Marta would have started yelling at both kids, exacerbating the stress of the situation. Instead, she took a deep breath and repeated her mantra: *the chaos is temporary*. After taking a moment to center herself, Marta approached the children calmly. Shortly after, Jonah and Tabitha followed the tone that Marta had set, and they, too, were able to regroup. Since she wasn't yelling, their anger and frustration did not continue to escalate, and instead, all three were able to regulate their emotions. They worked together to clean up the spilled juice and made a system for sharing the blocks.

What Is Mindful Parenting?

Mindfulness approaches encourage us to focus on the emotion and to *pause* before reacting. Instead of reacting automatically, we regulate our emotions and take the space we need to remain calm, keep our children calm, and problem-solve the situation.

Mindful parenting is an approach to parenting that incorporates the following themes:

1. ***Listening with Full Attention:*** Being aware of children's verbal and nonverbal cues can help us detect their intended meaning. Accurately interpreting children's cues leads to better communication and less conflict.

    Listening with full attention means paying close attention to both what children *are* and *are not* saying. It involves observing their body language, facial expressions, and tone of voice in order to better understand their intentions and meaning. Listening with full attention helps to create a safe and trusting environment for children to communicate and reduces the potential for conflict. Additionally, it allows adults to interpret children's cues, allowing for better communication and a better understanding of their needs.

2. ***Nonjudgmental Acceptance:*** Setting realistic expectations of children and accepting those limits is important. This also extends to being accepting of our emotional experiences, as well as our children's, and to do so nonjudgmentally.

3. ***Emotional Awareness:*** Strong emotions tend to elicit an automatic negative reaction. When we have emotional

awareness, we can make a more conscious decision on how to respond.

Emotional awareness is the ability to recognize, understand, and manage our own emotions in different situations, as well as to recognize and understand the emotions of others. This type of awareness is key for making conscious decisions about how to respond to various emotions. When we have emotional awareness, we are able to recognize the source of our emotions and the impact they have on our behavior. We can then take the time to assess the situation and make a decision on how to respond in a way that best meets our needs and goals. Additionally, emotional awareness can help us create stronger connections with others by allowing us to better understand how our emotions can impact others.

4. **Self-Regulation:** This refers to the ability to appropriately express and talk through big emotions instead of simply reacting.

5. **Compassion:** This refers to being compassionate about your child's viewpoint, even if you disagree with it.

These points do not mean that mindful parents do not experience negative emotions. Negative emotions are normal and valid. We are supposed to feel sad, angry, or disappointed. It's how we respond to the emotion that matters. If your child does something that angers you, and your automatic reaction is to start yelling, what happens next? Younger children may cry or become fearful, and older children may argue. All this type of reaction does is keep negative emotions and interactions in a never-ending loop.

How To Mindfully Parent a Child with ADHD

So far, I've made a convincing argument for the benefits of embarking on a mindfulness journey. How, then, do you make the transition then to mindful parenting? And what does it look like in practice?

There are multiple skills and practices that encompass mindfulness, many of which will be highlighted throughout this workbook. The upcoming section will address the core mindfulness practices and offer steps to begin your practice. It's important to note, however, that there are several roles that you, as the parent, will play.

First, as a novice, you learn and absorb as much as possible about this new topic. Secondly, as an apprentice, you practice and integrate these skills into your daily routine, and lastly, you will serve as a model for your child. Your child's involvement in this workbook will vary, depending on their age, temperament, and interest level. Regardless of how much of this workbook they are reading and practicing, your job will be to model using and applying these skills. Modeling mindfulness will help demonstrate the practices and encourage your child to learn, imitate, and incorporate these skills. Here are some tips to aid this process:

- Create a consistent, structured environment: Establishing a regular routine and predictable structure can help your child stay focused and organized. This includes setting realistic expectations, providing clear instructions, and helping them create a schedule that works for them.
- Cultivate patience: Mindful parenting involves being patient and understanding with your child. Remember that children with ADHD are often impulsive and have difficulty controlling their behavior.
- Show empathy: Acknowledge and validate your child's feelings, even if you don't agree with them. This will help them feel heard and understood.
- Use positive reinforcement: Praise your child when they make progress, no matter how small. This will help them feel encouraged and motivated to keep trying.
- Model mindfulness: Help your child learn to be mindful by practicing mindfulness techniques such as deep breathing exercises, body scans, and guided visualizations.
- Encourage physical activity: Exercise can help reduce symptoms of ADHD. Find activities that your child enjoys and encourage them to get active.

- Take breaks: Give yourself and your child frequent breaks throughout the day to decompress and reset. This can help your child stay focused and on task.

Make Your Needs a Priority

There is a direct link between self-care and mental health. Research shows that parents of children with behavior difficulties experience higher levels of both anxiety and depression, as well as, relatedly, overall family and marital conflict. This suggests that these parents have an even *higher* need for self-care practices since you can't effectively take care of others unless your own mental health is in check.

Besides the personal benefits of making your needs a priority, sharing this lesson with your children is also important. The best way to teach children the role of self-care in wellness is to model the behavior. This teaches children ways to promote long-term well-being by becoming aware of physical and emotional needs and handling future life stressors.

Lastly, ensuring good self-care habits is also important from a mindfulness perspective. Mindfulness practices encourage being fully present in each moment without distraction or judgment. This is difficult to do if we are not caring for our own physical and emotional well-being.

Develop a Calm New Approach to Tough Experiences

Parenting can be stressful and overwhelming, but mindfulness can help during challenging moments. The steps below can help create a state of calm. With practice, these can be used as a coping tool in a moment of distress.

- **Mindful Awareness**: Pay attention to the present moment and only the present moment. Use your five senses: What do you see right now? Hear? Smell? Feel? Taste?
- **Body Awareness**: Pay attention to the physical sensations you are experiencing. Take deep breaths and focus on your heartbeat or the sensation of your inhales and exhales.
- **Cognitive Awareness**: Keep your thoughts focused solely on what is true and happening right now. Also, consider how these thoughts relate to how you feel emotionally, right now.

Actively Listen to Your Child

Children tend to talk a lot, which can be overwhelming and, at times, annoying. However, active listening is a great tool to improve communication. When parents actively listen, children feel connected, understood, and supported. This willingness to listen translates into an opportunity for parents to help children explore, clarify, and learn appropriate ways to express their emotions and behaviors. Key behaviors in active listening include:

- **Empty Hands Listening**: This means giving your child 100% attention while speaking and having "empty hands," meaning not using your phone or cooking dinner while conversing.
- **Don't interrupt**: Let your child process as they speak, even if that means they are giving you a stream of consciousness or the conversation has gone tangentially.
- **Don't problem-solve**: Let your child know you are engaged and listening by reflecting on their emotional experience and offering support:

"That sounds like a terrible day!"

Reinforce Success with Praise and Rewards

As parents, we want to keep our children safe. Therefore, our natural inclination is to punish bad (or unsafe) behavior. However, learning and behavior theory tells us that the better approach to guiding children's behavior is to *positively reinforce* it, meaning to spend more time *rewarding the behavior we would like to see continued.* The key to positive reinforcement is that we are likely to perform the behavior again when we receive a reward for the behavior. Therefore, by rewarding children for what they do well, we increase their confidence and belief in themselves and their capabilities.

While punishments teach children what not to do, they do not necessarily teach them what they *should* do. Additionally, we

34

typically execute a punishment while angry, so in addition to taking away a privilege or object, you may also verbally punish the child; *I can't believe you did this! I'm so disappointed in you. Your brother never acts this way.* More often than not, the correct behavior isn't being learned; instead, children internalize some pretty negative messages.

Praise and rewards are powerful tools for reinforcing success. Praise can be verbal or nonverbal, such as a smile or a pat on the back. Rewards can be tangible or intangible, such as a special treat or recognition. Both can help to reinforce positive behaviors and help motivate people to want to achieve more. Praise and rewards can also help to build self-confidence and a sense of accomplishment. By providing both praise and rewards, we can help create a culture of success and can motivate others to strive for even better results.

Thoughtfully Set Consistent Boundaries

Whether boundaries are physical, mental, emotional, or time-based, they are important to create and maintain. Boundaries are important in all relationships. However, in children with ADHD, firm and healthy boundaries are critical because of their difficulty in self-regulating behaviors and emotions.

Boundaries allow kids to know their limits and can help create a routine. Rules and predictability can help reduce uncertainty, which in turn reduces anxiety.

Create and maintain your boundaries mindfully. Communicate your boundaries and be clear and specific about your expectations. Be mindful of your child's age and current level of functioning. Boundaries that are too rigid or do not consider your child's current difficulties will set them up for failure. It's OK to start small with attainable, realistic boundaries and gradually build from there.

Create Routines

A similar argument can be made for the benefits of creating routines. Routines help establish expectations, and most of us, including those with ADHD, respond better to structure and predictability. This helps create a sense of calm and reduces anxiety and conflict.

Like boundaries, the routine should be communicated and flexible. Being too rigid with your routine will lead to even more frustration and conflict.

Recall that one of our goals for mindfulness is nonjudgmental acceptance and setting realistic expectations. Acknowledge *both* your child's capabilities and challenges. They may need reminders about what comes next. Many children with ADHD benefit from transitional warnings: *We will start getting dressed in five minutes.* It may be helpful to let your children have a timer to keep track of time spent on-task. Young children can use the alarm to indicate that time is up; *when you hear the fun bells, it means playtime is over.* In my office, I often spend a few minutes letting children pick the sound of the alarm they want to hear. It is a great way to engage them in the task.

Practice Gratitude

Gratitude is a conscious effort to count our blessings, an important practice in mindfulness theory, and an important component of creating compassion. There is an exhaustive list of benefits related to a gratitude practice. The most relevant here include reducing toxic emotions, including aggression and frustration, and replacing them with a sense of calm. Research also shows that families that practice gratitude together have a stronger connection.

Start a daily gratitude practice where you name three things you are thankful for. When ready, expand this practice by finding something positive in a challenging situation. Aha! Parenting gives examples such as *Thank goodness she had this meltdown here instead of in the store; I'm getting better at dealing with his anger calmly; At least this came up now, so I can see how upset he is and address it.*

Your child likely has some troubles that you are constantly working on improving – behaviorally, emotionally, socially, or academically. These problem areas are likely talked about daily, with a constant focus on trying to make progress, asking for updates and reviewing missteps and blunders. While this is all for your child's benefit, this constant focus on their shortcomings can also negatively impact them. It can cause a lack of motivation to do better and feelings of defensiveness and demoralization. Kids can start internalizing that they are not good enough or that everything they do is wrong.

Identify and Focus on Your Child's Unique Strengths

While you must encourage your child to improve problem areas, ensure you are also praising and cultivating areas of strength. This will boost self-confidence and self-esteem and help your child develop a more positive self-image: all of which will encourage your child to continue honing these skills *(remember the benefits of praise and positive reinforcement!)*

Here are a few tips to help you focus on your child's strengths:

- **Find the strengths**. Strengths can be what your child is good at, but they may also be things they are interested in, passionate about, or enjoy.
- **Provide experiences to practice the strength**.

38

- **Make sure you praise the *effort*,** not just the *outcome*: *You worked hard on that science project!*
- **Document successes**. Keep a list of your child's achievements and successes, no matter how small. Talk about what contributed to each success – these may be additional strengths. Review the list often and remind your child of their accomplishments. This will reinforce their self-image.

How to Set Shared Expectations and Goals

Talking to your child about your goals for this program is important. Open communication is vital to your children feeling respected so that they understand that their thoughts and perspectives matter. It can also help with cooperation and motivation to commit to a program like this. Open communication helps build a child's self-confidence and can promote a healthy parent-child relationship.

When talking to your child about your goals for this program, it is important to explain why it is important for them to participate. Help them understand the benefits of the program, such as developing skills such as self-discipline, learning to work both independently and with others, and gaining a deeper understanding of the subject you are studying.

Explain how it will help them to excel in school and in life. Invite their input and ideas and let them know that their participation is valued. Ask them what they think they can do to help make the program successful. Finally, emphasize the importance of commitment and hard work and that you are there to support them every step of the way.

Goal setting with an ADHD diagnosis can be challenging, but as mentioned in Chapter 1, there are strengths, or superpowers, associated with ADHD. Familiarizing yourself with your child's strengths can make it easier to set goals together. For example, children who hyper-focus or are good at focusing on the here and now may be motivated by smaller, short-term goals.

The 6C's can help you with expectations and goal setting with your child. Parent and child should:

- Have a *conversation* about goals and the parent's expectations with the child, allowing providing feedback.
- Parent and child should then *collaborate* to set goals together.
- The goals should be *clear*.
- The goals should be *consistent* and attainable for your child's age and abilities.
- Provide *choices* for your child so they feel a part of the process. Younger children can choose rewards for a job well done; older children can help set a timeline for goal attainment that feels realistic and manageable.

- Finally, *check in* with them along the way, offering support and talking about the process and their progress. Be flexible, and make changes or adaptations as needed.

How to Get Your Child to Participate?

Mindful parenting, generally, and this workbook, specifically, is most effective when the parent can get the child to collaborate and work together. This can be arduous, especially for spirited children.

The best approach to getting your child on board is using open communication. I encourage parents to tell their kids the age-appropriate version of the truth from an early age. Explain to your child where you think you are struggling and how this workbook can help.

- *I want to work on being angry less often.*
- *I'd like us to try to work better together.*
- *I want to learn some tricks to help me when I feel frustrated.*
- *I want to find ways to help make homework easier.*

Open communication goes both ways: ask your child if there is anything they would like to work on, either their personal goals or shared goals between parent and child.

What if your child refuses to participate? Much like a child refusing therapy, we do not want to force them into any treatment.

41

Therapeutic-style interventions are not a punishment and should not be viewed as such. These types of systems require active engagement from the participant to work. Unfortunately, there will not be many benefits if you force your child into participating. If your child is refusing, the best course of action from here is for you to work on building your mindfulness practice on your own. Hopefully, your child will become curious as you start to model healthier, calmer approaches to your parenting. They may even start to mimic some of the strategies that you are using, especially once they see they have a positive benefit.

Considering Other Treatment Options for ADHD

After an ADHD diagnosis, many families consider medications to help treat symptoms. The decision to start a medication regimen for your child is a big one. Most parents I speak to are hesitant to consider medications. When pressed for their reasons, I find that they usually do not know enough about the class of drugs that treat ADHD to make an informed decision. I always suggest to parents: do your research, ask some questions, and then decide.

Research shows that ADHD treatment options are extremely safe and that many children show marked improvements in various areas of functioning. For example, in 2020, a large research study found that treating ADHD with medication yielded positive academic outcomes, with a decreased likelihood of developing mood disorders, accidents, and injuries.

Many children with ADHD also have other coexisting diagnoses that may require treatment. Some children may benefit from other treatment strategies, such as psychotherapy, social skills training, family therapy, or occupational therapy. Work collaboratively with your medical treatment team to determine the best options for your child.

Lastly, as with all medications, there is the risk of side effects to consider.

Before deciding, speak to your child's doctor, or schedule a consultation with a child psychiatrist to learn about the different medications, and what the benefits and risks would be.

Some questions to consider:

- Is the medication suggested a stimulant or non-stimulant?
- What are the potential benefits?
- What are the possible side effects?
- What will this medication not help with?
- Is there another treatment option that would be a better choice, either on its own or in conjunction with this medication?

Embracing Mindfulness as a Parent

Congratulations! You have made it through Part 1 and the foundational components of your mindfulness journey. Hopefully, you are moving forward with a firmer understanding of what ADHD is and how it affects your child, yourself, your home life, and your family.

It is very likely that in reading about the foundations of mindfulness, you recall moments in the past when you may have reacted negatively to your child. This is a great opportunity to begin to apply mindfulness skills. Start by *acknowledging* that you were operating from a different emotional place. You did not *yet* have the tools to parent mindfully. Use your *nonjudgmental acceptance* skills, and do not judge your past reactions.

Develop a mantra that you can tell yourself in the future if you start ruminating about the past and experiencing feelings of guilt and shame. Remind yourself that you are learning *emotional awareness* and *self-regulation*. Helpful thoughts that can be used as mantras may be: *I am learning; I am growing; I am allowed to make mistakes. I can forgive myself for my mistakes.*

You may also doubt your ability to maintain calmness in the future when triggered. It is normal to feel apprehensive about mastering and applying a new skill. While this will not be a perfect journey, mindfulness is a skill anyone can learn with practice. Keep an open mind, be patient, practice, and be kind and compassionate towards yourself and your child as you learn healthier ways to navigate this journey together.

Key Takeaways

This chapter discussed and explained how mindful parenting approaches incorporate listening with full attention, using nonjudgmental acceptance, developing emotional awareness and self-regulation, and doing all things compassionately. We reviewed parenting practices that encompass these core elements of mindfulness.

- Make your needs a priority: your self-care and mental health are directly related and positively impact your children.
- Use mindful, body and cognitive awareness to approach tough experiences
- Actively listen to your child
- Positive reinforcement is more effective than punishment
- Set consistent boundaries and routines
- Create a gratitude practice
- Praise and cultivate your child's areas of strength
- Use the 6C's to goal-set with your child:
  - Have a conversation
  - Collaborate
  - Set clear and consistent goals
  - Provide choices
  - Check-in along the way
  - Be a role model

Part II:

Transforming Yourself Into A Mindful Parent

Now that you have a basic understanding of ADHD as well as a foundational idea of mindfulness theory, we can dive into the core of our journey. Part II will focus on how to incorporate this new knowledge into an overall daily practice.

In Chapter 3, we will integrate self-care into our mindfulness practice. We will do this by learning proper deep breathing techniques, cultivating gratitude, and practicing mindfulness throughout our daily routine. In Chapter 4, we will learn effective ways to manage emotions during chaotic times as parents. The exercises teach us to acknowledge and accept our negative feelings, to challenge our negative thoughts, and to accept and let go of the things that are not in our control. In Chapter 5, we will apply these skills to parenting, as we will focus on positive praise, communication, and rewards.

Within these next pages, there is a wealth of powerful information. Take your time, read slowly, and allow yourself to digest, process, apply skills and practice. Mastery of each skill will take time!

Chapter 3:
Make Your Needs a Priority

Introduction

Self-care is one of the most essential components of good mental health. We cannot begin to care for others if our own needs aren't being met. I always relate this idea to emergency produces when flying: we are told to adjust our own oxygen mask before helping others.

In addition, in times of stress, or when we are feeling sad or overwhelmed, self-care is the first thing that the majority of us sacrifice. Think about your New Year's Resolutions from the past few years: *I'm going to get into a good workout routine! I'm going to go to spin class every week!* Think back to reasons why you didn't maintain these goals: work was busy, the kids were stressful – it was easier to cancel that plan, rather than have one more thing on the to do list.

In a recent study, parents of children with ADHD identified four primary sources of stress: they referred to their children's behavior as a "wrecking ball," they struggled to cope with the "war at home," their relationships with their siblings and spouse "didn't survive," and it was "goddamn hard work." While everyone can benefit from self-care, when this is your reality, self-care is even more important.

The mental health trifecta is a good starting point for self-care.

A strong network of
friends and family.

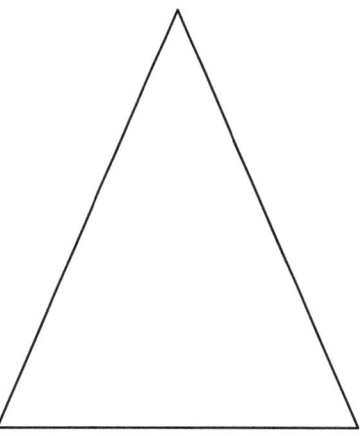

An exercise
regimen.

Hobbies or pastimes
that you enjoy.

Think of these elements as the foundation for a good self-care system. Once these are in place, we can begin to add on mindfulness practices that will elevate your overall wellbeing.

Case Study

Both of Alicia's preteens have been diagnosed with ADHD, hyperactive – impulsive subtype. Her elderly parents also live close by and require frequent care. Juggling multiple responsibilities between work, home life, children, and her parents has created constant anxiety for Alicia. She is always overwhelmed and exhausted. By the time dinner is over, she has no energy or patience to argue with her children about homework. As a result, the nighttime routine has become yelling and fighting, as Alicia's children resist doing homework, or they have lost or left at school something integral to getting their assignments done.

To better manage her feelings of frustration and overwhelm, Alicia began practicing mindfulness techniques such as staying present in the current moment and nonjudgmental acceptance. Alicia learned how to shift her priorities to be sure her own needs were being met, as well as relaxation skills to help de-stress and respond more effectively to stressful situations. The pressures she faces are the same as before and will not change in the immediate future, but she is now better prepared to cope with them. These skills are also helping her to model for her children how to be more tolerant and compassionate, as well as better ways to care for their own mental and emotional health.

Affirmation

"I am a work in progress."

Being mindful – or aware – of the impact that our thoughts have on our emotions, behaviors, and intentions is critical to a successful mindfulness practice. Affirmations help with this awareness and help to define focus. They can be extremely beneficial in maintaining both motivation and an encouraging outlook on our mindfulness journey.

Some of my favorites that can help with self-care include:

I believe in myself and my ability to succeed.

I am a work in progress.

I deserve peace and love.

I am inhaling peace and exhaling stress.

I deserve to be kind to myself.

I am in the process of becoming the best version of myself.

What affirmation resonates with you? Much like your mantra from Chapter 1, your affirmation is something to pair with deep breathing. Add your affirmation to your self-care routine: say it to yourself a few times upon waking up and before going to bed. Repeat it to yourself throughout the day as necessary to maintain positive thinking patterns and stop negative thoughts.

Self-Care Checklist

Self-care practices can affect all areas of your life. Below are some self-care strategies that you may already be using.

Rate each item on the frequency that you are performing it. The goal is to gain insight on your current patterns and on the areas of your life that may need more attention.

Rate each item on a scale of:

- I do this rarely or not at all
- I do this sometimes
- I do this often

Use an X to indicate activities that you would like to do more of.

Personal Self-Care

	Rating
• *Foster relationships*	
• *Go on dates*	
• *Relax*	
• *Plan*	
• *Set goals*	
• *Daydream*	
• *Do something you enjoy that you are not necessarily good at*	
• *Dance*	

• *Total Score:*

Physical Self-Care

	Rating
• *Exercise 3x a week*	
• *Sleep well 80% of the time*	
• *Eat well 80% of the time*	
• *Go to medical appointments when needed*	
• *Go to medical appointments for prevention*	
• *Wear clothes that help me feel good about myself*	
• *Take care of personal hygiene*	
• *Rest when sick*	
• *Total Score:*	

Emotional Self-Care

	Rating
• *Take time off from work, school, or obligations*	
• *Practice gratitude*	
• *Laugh*	
• *Taking space from screens (phones, laptops, TV)*	
• *Ask for help when needed*	
• *Talk about my problems*	
• *Allow myself to express emotion*	
• *Express my feelings by journaling*	
• *Total Score:*	

Social Self-Care

Particulars	Rating
• *Spend time with family or friends*	
• *Spend time with my partner*	
• *Reach out to friends and family who are far away*	
• *Meet new people*	
• *Volunteer*	
• *Take a break from social media*	
• *Honor your boundaries*	
• *Cultivate a new hobby*	
• *Total Score:*	

Spiritual Self-Care

Particulars	Rating
• *Meditate*	
• *Have a mantra or affirmation*	
• *Pray*	
• *Spend time in nature*	
• *Read inspiring material*	
• *Spend time reflecting*	
• *Appreciate art*	
• *Practice forgiveness*	
• *Total Score:*	

Professional Self-Care

Particulars	Rating
• *Recognize and celebrate my accomplishments*	
• *Learn new things related to my field*	
• *Take breaks during work*	
• *Set healthy boundaries outside of the workday*	
• *Say no*	
• *Do job tasks that are rewarding or interesting*	
• *Build professional relationships*	
• *Time to truly disconnect*	
• *Total Score:*	

Take a moment to think about how you did on the Self-Care Checklist and how you currently care for yourself. For each category, higher scores indicate a greater frequency of self-care behaviors. Do you recognize areas where you are doing well? Areas that you could improve? Can you think of additional activities in each category that you would enjoy? What activities did you indicate that you would like to do more of?

_____

_____

_____

Reflection: Building and Improving Self-Care Habits

Let's take a moment to reflect on additional ways to build and improve your self-care habits.

Tip: Remember that engaging in unhealthy activities do not count as self-care. Short-term relief can be attained through substance abuse or binge eating, for example, but these behaviors often lead to greater problems in the long run.

Consider the following, and write your responses in the space provided:

1. What advice do I give others that I should follow?

2. What type of movement feels best for my body?

_____

3. What excites me?

_____

4. What makes me feel calm?

_____

5. What makes my heart feel full?

_____

6. Which habits negatively impact my ability to engage in self-care?

_____

7. What is something I can tell myself to use as a reminder of the importance of self-care?

_____

Self-Care Tracker

Track your self-care activities on the calendar provided. Over the next few weeks, keep a log of how often you do each activity.

Self-care goals, like most goals, shouldn't be too ambitious. Setting a goal to exercise every day, for instance, sounds great, but the reality is that there will invariably be obstacles that prevent you from accomplishing this goal. Goals that are unrealistic quickly become demotivating because you are setting yourself up for failure.

Tip: When setting your goals, keep MAMAS in mind!

Goals should be:

*M*easurable: How will you track progress? (*The chart below is one way!*)

*A*ttainable: Is the goal realistic?

*M*onitored: As you achieve milestones, make sure you acknowledge and celebrate them!

*A*djustable: Change the goal as necessary – it's OK to break a goal down into smaller, more easily achieved steps!

*S*imple: Be specific, but do not overthink the goal you are working towards!

My goals are:

1._____
2. _____
3. _____
4. _____
5. _____

Set weekly self-care goals using the chart below and keep tabs on your progress.

Self-care Goal:	Sun	Mon	Tues	Wed	Thurs	Fri	Sat
Goal 1:							
Goal 2:							
Goal 3:							

*Tip: It's not necessary to practice each form of self-care every single day. This is **unattainable.** I recommend the 80 percent rule: are you engaging in some form of self-care on 80 percent of the days? Over time, you will notice patterns in what self-care routines work best for you, and can **adjust** your goals accordingly.*

Mindful Breathing

Now that we have laid the framework for self-care, we can start adding mindfulness practices. At numerous times throughout this workbook, I have referenced "deep breathing." This is such an important cornerstone of mindfulness theory that I want to review the proper technique.

The practice of deep breathing is often linked to anxiety interventions because of the role that the breath plays in the nervous system. When we feel anxious, our sympathetic nervous system is activated, which causes our heart rate to quicken, our breath to become shallow, our core temperature to rise, and our hands to become sweaty. With just a few slow, deep breaths, we can stimulate the parasympathetic nervous system, which decreases heart rate, releases muscle tension, and stops perspiration.

Deep breathing is powerful, but mindfulness theory takes it one step further. Mindfulness theory believes these paced inhales and exhales cause breathing to act as an anchor, something that commands our attention and keeps us in the present rather than dwelling on the past or the future.

Deep breathing is breathing that comes from deep in our *diaphragms*, as opposed to our chest. Oftentimes, when we are feeling anxious, our breathing becomes shorter and more shallow. This panicked-style breathing is what we are trying to avoid. This type of breathing does not allow our lungs to fill with air and can actually create feelings of anxiety. A good mental image of breathing from your chest is how anxiety is depicted in movies: the actor is taking short rapid breaths and is often breathing into a paper bag.

What we are striving for is referred to as *diaphragmatic breathing*. This deep abdominal breathing engages the diaphragm, pushes out the stomach, and fills the lungs fully with air. This then can lower blood pressure, decrease heart rate, relax muscles, decrease stress, and increase energy levels.

Let's practice the proper breathing technique

Step 1: Awareness of Breath

- Place one hand on your chest and the other on your abdomen, just under your ribcage.
- Take a deep breath through your nose, slowly counting to five.
- Imagine your stomach slowly filling like a balloon, keeping your chest still.
- The hand on your abdomen should be pushed out as the stomach expands.
- Hold your breath for another count of 5.
- Slowly exhale through your mouth as you slowly count to 5.
- Gently contract your stomach muscles to completely let go of any remaining air.
- The hand on your abdomen should move closer to you as the stomach retracts.
- Imagine your stomach like a balloon slowly emptying.
- Repeat this cycle 5 times.

Once you feel comfortable, you can progress to mindful breathing exercises, such as the following:

Step 2:

During Box Breathing, you'll match your breaths to the imaginary drawing of a four-sided box (or square). Some individuals visualize a box. Others, imagine tracing each line, or side of the box, pairing one line with each step of the exercise.

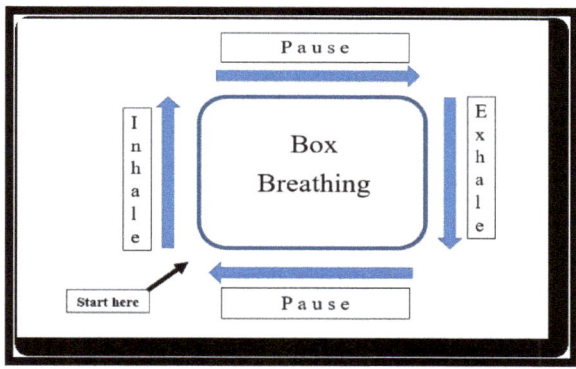

Step 1 / Line 1: Inhale through the nose for a count of 4.

Step 2 / Line 2: Hold your breath for a count of 4.

Step 3 / Line 3: Exhale through the mouth for a count of 4.

Step 4 / Line 4: Hold your breath for a count of 4.

Repeat.

Step 3: Incorporate your Affirmation or Mantra

- Recall your mantra from Chapter 1 and/or your affirmation from above.
- Follow the deep breathing steps above.
- Continue breathing slowly as you begin to chant your mantra. You can say it out loud or to yourself silently.
- Your mantra and breathing will eventually fall into a rhythm.

Incorporating Your Senses

The most common complaint I hear from my patients when they are first learning mindfulness skills and meditation is that they "can't stop thinking" or that they become distracted by their thoughts as they try to focus on their breathing. This is normal! If your mind wanders while doing any of these exercises, instead of getting frustrated or giving up, simply bring your thoughts back to the exercise and pick up wherever you left off.

When first learning mindfulness, to help prevent distraction, it can be helpful to practice exercises that are a bit more cognitively engaging. One technique I find helpful is to incorporate deep breathing with your five senses. In this exercise, describe the current moment using only your sense.

For example, I am currently working in a coffee shop.

First, I get into a calm pattern of inhales and exhales. Then, I look around. I *see* students from the nearby university standing in line, ordering their coffee. I *see* numerous students hunched over laptops, typing furiously, or reading a textbook with a coffee cup in one hand. I *smell* the coffee grinds and cinnamon and sugar coming from the pastry counter across the room. I *hear* chattering from the table to the left of mine, two friends talking about something that happened over the weekend. I *hear* a parent to the right of me singing a nursery rhyme to her small toddler. I *feel* the hard keyboard keys under my fingers. I *feel* the fur of my snow boots around my ankles (it's cold in NYC today!). I *feel* the hard seat under me. I taste the bitterness of my coffee when I take a sip. I *taste* the buttery sweetness of my croissant.

This meditation could also be much more descriptive. I could describe to myself what the students in line were wearing, including the color of their scarves and backpacks. I could describe to myself, in detail, what the coffee shop looks like, including the art on the walls and the tables and chairs.

Tip: Remember, mindfulness meditation is to keep anchored to this present moment. While I am being mindful, I am not thinking about what happened this morning or all of the chores I must do after dinner.

Your turn!

Using as many of your 5 senses as you can, describe where you are right now.

- I see

  _____

- I hear

  _____

- I smell

  _____

- I taste

  _____

- I feel

  _____

Mindfulness can:

Change your brain chemistry, particularly in the areas of memory, learning, and emotion regulation

Increase compassion towards those suffering

Increase pain tolerance

Help with decision making

Increase creativity

Lead to better sex, particularly for women

Increase athletic performance

Motivation and Mindfulness

Keeping your interest and enthusiasm levels high is crucial when acquiring new knowledge. We need motivation to plan for the future, pursue our passions, adjust our habits, and develop our abilities. We've spent some time talking about how mindfulness can help you take care of your own mental health and cope with the challenges of ADHD.

Mindfulness, however, has far-reaching effects beyond these. Here are some more exciting benefits of mindfulness practice to keep your enthusiasm up.

A variety of people, including children, the critically ill, pregnant women, therapists, patients of therapists, and police officers, have benefited from practicing mindfulness, according to studies.

Finding Mindfulness Everywhere

We can use the power of mindfulness at any time to anchor us to the moment that we are in. Think about mundane tasks that you do throughout the day where maybe you operate on autopilot. These are excellent opportunities to engage in a mindfulness meditation. Next time you are waiting in line, washing dishes, or commuting to work, try describing to yourself what you see or incorporating your senses to anchor yourself to that given moment.

Mindful eating is a great way to start practicing mindfulness. Think about the last time you enjoyed a bowl of popcorn or a box of raisins. Most likely, you grabbed a handful, popped them in your mouth, and chewed for a few seconds, and then grabbed for more. Did you actually taste the raisin or the popcorn? Could you tell the difference between the textures? Intentionally focusing on our sensory experiences and grounding ourselves in the here and now is a key component of practicing mindful eating. Let's try it out with a bag of pre-popped or freshly popped popcorn.

- *Begin* grounding yourself by taking a comfortable seat with your feet flat on the floor. Eliminate distractions, such as TV, laptops, and phones.
- *Take* a few deep breaths and start to notice a sense of calm spread within you.

- *Bring* your attention to a bowl of popcorn and observe with curiosity. Look at the popcorn as if you have never seen it before. Notice the color, shape, texture, and size. What do you see?
- *Pick* up a kernel, holding it between your fingers. Feel the texture, the temperature, the ridges. What do the "petals" of the kernel feel like? What else do you notice?
- *Take* a deep inhale and smell the kernel. Close your eyes and think of the scent. Is it corn? Butter? Salt? Does the smell cause you to recall any memories of another time you were eating popcorn?
- *Now*, place the kernel on your tongue. Without chewing or swallowing, take a moment to note what the texture feels like. What do you taste? What is the temperature of the kernel? Is it savory, sweet, or salty?
- *Take* a bite. Notice any changes in texture and taste.
- *Start* chewing slowly until the kernel completely dissolves. What sound does the kernel make as you chew?
- *When* you are ready, swallow the kernel, but take note of the path it takes from your mouth to your throat and to your stomach.
- *Is* there any sensation or taste lingering in your mouth? Take a moment to connect with your body and take note of your experience at this moment.

Finding Gratitude

Chapter 1 introduced the idea of gratitude and discussed the many positive benefits of developing a gratitude practice, including reducing toxic emotions and replacing them with a sense of calm.

Research has linked gratitude not only to improved mental health but also to improvements in physical health, relationships, sleep, empathy, resilience, and self-esteem. Let's make a list of everything you have to be thankful for. This can be people, places, pets, opportunities, and experiences. Consider moments such as the great feedback you received on a project last week, your child's team winning the soccer game, or seeing two birds flying together in the wind on a sunny afternoon.

What are some things you are grateful for?

1. _____
2. _____
3. _____
4. _____
5. _____

Refer back to this list whenever you feel the need for a general reminder of the good in your life or in moments when you are feeling down.

Gratitude Meditation

A gratitude meditation, like keeping a gratitude journal, can help you retrain your brain to focus on the positive things in life. ***Tip:*** You can pair any of your gratitude lists with deep breathing or just using the mantra, *I am grateful for…*

Get into a comfortable positive, either sitting or lying down. Start with a few long, deep breaths. With each exhale, visualize the tension leaving your body. Once you've found a comfortable breathing pattern, it's time to start thinking about what you're thankful for. As each gratitude appears, visualize yourself saying "thank you."

Feel gratitude for your mind and how it lets you think, dream, plan and reminisce. Say thank you.

- Feel gratitude for your heart, and how it lets you love and care for your close ones. Say thank you.
- Feel gratitude for your body and how it lets you navigate life. Say thank you.
- Feel gratitude for your food and how it nourishes and energizes you. Say thank you.
- Feel gratitude for your network of family and friends and how they support you. Say thank you.
- Feel gratitude for your work for challenging you and giving you purpose. Say thank you.

- Feel gratitude for the sunshine for providing warmth and nourishment. Say thank you.
- Feel gratitude for the lessons that you've learned that provide opportunities for growth. Say thank you.
- Feel gratitude for the cathartic opportunity for laughter. Say thank you.

Mindfulness Reflection

Now that you have been introduced to several mindfulness practices let's reflect on the experience.

1. Which mindfulness skill(s) did you like best?

_____

_____

2. For each skill, describe what the practice felt like. Did you experience a decrease in anxiety, stress, or physical tension? Did it help to create a moment of calm?

_____

_____

3. Which mindfulness skills would you like to continue?

_____

_____

4. How can you plan to keep mindfulness in your life going forward?

73

_____

_____

Key Takeaways

We can all agree that we can have the best intentions when it comes to breathing practices and meditations, but the second we are stressed or busy or out of routine, these self-care habits are the first thing to be cut out. In the moments we need our self-care routine the *most,* we are so quick to dismiss them. As parents of children with ADHD, the benefits of self-care do not only benefit us, but they benefit our children as well. They help us remain calm, to take a moment before reacting, and to respond appropriately. Our most important relationships – those with our children and spouses – will significantly benefit from us taking the time to maintain self-care. It also allows us to model healthy mental health habits and coping strategies. Use your self-care checklist to identify areas where you should improve your self-care habits.

- Goals should be MAMAS: Measurable, Attainable, Monitored, Adjustable, and Simple.
- Diaphragmatic breathing helps decrease heart rate and stress.
- Find mindfulness practice everywhere by incorporating your five senses, applying them to eating, or using them to stay present.

- Formal gratitude practices, such as journaling or meditation, can have a positive effect on our physical health, relationships, sleep, and self-esteem.

Chapter 4
Reacting Calmly to Chaos as a Parent

Introduction

This chapter will help you learn to stay calm, focused and in control in the face of the chaos and challenges of parenting a child with ADHD. In order to accomplish this, the chapter lays out mindfulness practices that focus on building awareness to our emotional states, so that we can respond instead of react in a calm way. We start with creating an affirmation for this chapter, and then add proper deep breathing techniques. From there, we will do a Progressive Muscle Relaxation which allows us to recognize the difference between a relaxed and tense muscle state.

Our focus then shifts to becoming mindful of our emotions and thinking patterns. The ACA Method is an approach that helps us to *acknowledge, find control* and *accept* our negative emotions. We will become aware of our negative thought patterns, challenge them, and ultimately learn to let go of them. Each skill listed here builds on the previous skill, however, they can each be used independently. Practice building your mastery of each one, paying close attention to what works best for you.

Case Study

Sam has experienced intense bouts of anxiety for as long as he can remember. After stopping and starting with various therapists over the years, he eventually learned about mindfulness, but fell out of practice in recent years. Sam is now married and is a father of three. Jorge, his middle child, is 7 and has ADHD. Sam would describe their relationship as challenging. Jorge has trouble following directions and usually needs to be reminded multiple times before he takes action. He has a reputation for being a bit of a class clown and for constantly getting out of his seat, both of which get him into trouble at school. Sam gets irritated at home because of the length of time it takes Jorge to do things like get dressed, put on his coat, and load the dishwasher after dinner.

Sam has recently returned to mindfulness as a way to cope with his emotional stress and frustration. Sam found progressive muscle relaxations to be particularly beneficial and began incorporating them into his routine a few times a week. Recently, when trying to get Jorge to change into his pajamas as bedtime, Jorge began challenging him. Normally, Sam would immediately get frustrated, would start raising his voice, and would only get Jorge to comply because he was yelling. Instead, without thinking, Jorge found himself exhaling deeply. He then was able to talk to Jorge instead of responding angrily.

Affirmation

Recall from Chapter 3, we paired a self-care affirmation with deep breathing. We will do the same here.

I am in the calm in the chaos.

Is there a parenting affirmation that resonates with you?

Even with chaos, my house is filled with love.

We all struggle sometimes, but we love and support each other.

We are focusing on progress, not perfection.

Parenting Reflection

We are mindfully parenting when instead of *reacting* emotionally to our children's actions, we *respond* more thoughtfully. Being mindful and pausing before acting allows for a more considered response.

Recall a time when you had a hard time maintaining composure with your child.

1. Can you identify what caused you to become angry?

_____

2. Do you typically react this way?

_____

3. What were you thinking in that moment?

_____

4. How did you feel?

_____

5. When else have you felt this way?

_____

6. How did you feel afterwards?

_____

Mindful Pause

A mindful pause is achieved by stopping what you are doing and taking a moment to silence the outside noise and any inner thoughts and instead seeking a moment of peace and calm. Research has found that taking a mindful pause helps the nervous system regroup and find balance. This pause helps you to *respond* instead of *react*. With practice, the mindful pause will become a natural step that you take when in a moment of chaos. It will help ground and calm your emotions, helping you become more adept at responding rationally rather than emotionally in challenging circumstances.

To practice a mindful pause, get into a comfortable position, feet flat on the floor, fingers loosely in your lap.

Close your eyes, and over a series of slow deep breaths, bring your attention to the various rhythms of your body, such as your heart rate, your inhales and exhales.

With each exhale, notice there is a little more stillness, a little calmer, and a little quieter.

Try practicing this pause every day for a week so that your mind and body will know how to appropriately implement this skill when distressed.

Progressive Muscle Relaxation

Related to the idea of a mindful pause is the ability to recognize when your emotions manifest as tension in your body. We all do it: when stressed or overwhelmed, most of us tend to hold it physically in our body in the form of muscle tension. We may clench our jaws or tense our necks and shoulders. We often are not aware that we are holding the tension. It is tremendously easier to acknowledge the presence of negative emotions when we can recognize the physical tension we are holding in our bodies. A progressive muscle relaxation helps to do just that: it focuses on pairing deep breaths with tensing and relaxing various muscle groups. With this practice, your body will learn to better recognize and manage the physical effects of stress. You will learn to identify the difference between a tensed and relaxed muscle and will be able to relax it at the first sign of tension.

Have a seat or stretch out on the floor, whichever is more relaxing. Close your eyes and breathe deeply and slowly. Feel yourself beginning to enter a state of calm.

For each muscle group, tense the muscle on the inhale, and hold the tension for a count of five. Focus on slowly letting go of the tension in that muscle as you exhale for five seconds.

Use the table below to work through each muscle group. Tense and relax each muscle group twice before moving on to the next one.

Muscle Group – How to Tense It

- Hands – Clench into fists, then outstretch fingers
- Wrists – Pull backward towards your arms, then release
- Biceps – Flex into a muscle, then release
- Shoulders – Shrug towards your ears and hold, then release
- Jaw – Clench your teeth, then release
- Mouth – Open wide and hold, then release
- Nose – Scrunch and hold, then release
- Eyes – Open wide and hold, then release
- Forehead – Lift your eyebrows high and hold, then release
- Back – Arch and hold, then release
- Stomach – Clench your abdominal muscles and hold, then release

- Hips and Buttocks – Squeeze your gluteus muscles and hold, then release
- Thighs – Clench your thigh muscle and hold, then release
- Calf – Clench your calf muscle and hold, then release
- Hamstrings – Stretch your leg out straight and point your toes towards your face, then release
- Feet – Scrunch your toes and hold, then release
- Toes – Stretch them wide and hold, then release

Take a deep breath in and tense your entire body for a count of 5. Exhale and slowly relax. To end the meditation, slowly open your eyes. Stretch out your muscles as needed and enjoy the feeling of relaxation.

Introducing the ACA Method
(Acknowledge, Control, Accept)

When we feel negative emotions, the automatic response is often to just make them go away and to avoid them because it is painful to be in pain. Ignoring emotions does not make them go away. You may not want to feel bad (no one does!), but it is important that you acknowledge the negative emotion, because the feeling is real and valid!

Think back over the past week. What negative emotions did you feel, and why? Rate each emotion's intensity on a scale of 1 (mild) to 10 (extremely intense).

Tip: *Often, in hindsight, it is easy to dismiss or diminish the intensity of the emotion that we feel. Keep this fact in mind and try to be honest with yourself about how you truly felt at that moment.*

When _____ happened,
I was feeling_____.
Physical symptoms included_____.

When _____ happened,
I was feeling_____.
Physical symptoms included_____.

When _____ happened,
I was feeling_____.
Physical symptoms included_____.

Letting Go of Control

Understanding what we can and cannot control is a common topic in therapy. When we feel powerless or as though we are losing control, we may feel scared or anxious. For example, we cannot control if we get a job, but we can control how much we prepare for the interview. In parenting, there are a lot of things we do not have control over. We can provide for our children. We can love them,

83

support them and give them wonderful opportunities. However, we cannot control their behavior. We can teach them respect and manners, but we cannot control if others do not like our children. DO not forget that *we cannot control the situation, but we can control how we respond to it*.

Unfortunately, we do not have control over how situations ultimately turn out, or other people, but we are always in control of our responses: our words, decisions and behaviors. By shifting our focus to what is within our control, we will help limit our worry and instead focus it on more productive behavior.

Sean Covey, in his book, The 7 Habits of Highly Effective People, introduced the concept of a "circle of control" to help illustrate this very idea. In the circle below, try to draw aspects of your life that are in and out of your control. For example, outside of the circle, list things that you do not have control over, such as your workload or other people's opinions. Within the circle, write down the things you do have control over, such as how you spend your free time, how you treat your children, and how well you take care of yourself. Try to reflect on things that happen in the dynamics inside your home: what is within your control? What is not?

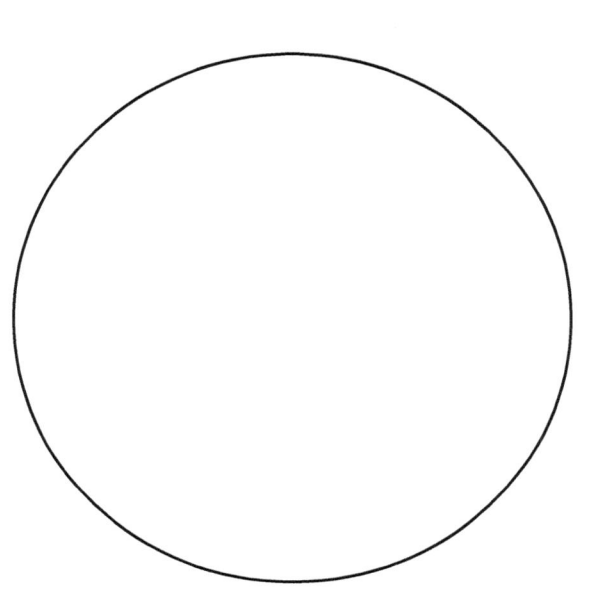

Emotional Acceptance

Our willingness and ability to accept and experience unpleasant emotions is called emotional acceptance. Acceptance allows us to accept the reality of a situation. Note that it does not include resignation or approval. We do not have to like or enjoy that we are feeling sad in order to accept that a particular circumstance made us sad. It takes less mental and physical energy to accept something rather than to deny or suppress our feelings about it. Lastly, when you allow yourself to feel a negative emotion, it tends to lose the power it has over you.

What emotions do you typically try to avoid?

_____

Why is this emotion uncomfortable for you?

_____

What can you do to help accept this emotion the next time you experience it?

_____

Tracking Negative Thoughts

Part of being mindful is developing an awareness of the way that we think, paying particular attention to the kinds of thoughts that we are experiencing. Oftentimes these negative thoughts are automatic and negatively skew our perception of the world. We accept these thoughts as absolute truths, and in doing so, we often trigger ourselves to feel angry, anxious or depressed. The next exercise will help you increase awareness of your thinking patterns and then to challenge these thoughts. Thought challenging is a simple yet effective technique that helps you to consider alternative perspectives.

Recognizing Negative Thought Patterns

When paying attention to your thoughts, there are several types of negative thoughts to be on the lookout for:

1. *All or Nothing Thinking: Thinking only in terms of extremes. You may see your child as either being good or bad, with no gray area in between.*
2. *Catastrophizing: Expecting the worst-case scenario in any situation, no matter how unlikely. My child is home late; he must have gotten into an accident.*
3. *Emotional Reasoning: The belief that the way you feel is indicative of reality. I feel like a bad parent, therefore, I must be a bad parent.*
4. *Mind-Reading: Assuming you know what other people are thinking. She thinks I am not a good parent.*
5. *Self-Labeling: Referring to yourself by a negative trait, usually based on a single experience. I am lazy.*
6. *Should(s): Should statements are rules and expectations you hold yourself or others too, that are usually unrealistic and not based on anything logical. I should be able to handle this.*
7. *What-If Thinking: Future-oriented thoughts about possible outcomes. They only take the negative into consideration. What if my child gets the same math teacher this year? What if my child continues to struggle in math? What if my child can't get into a good college because of their math grades?*

Tracking and Challenging Negative Thoughts

Negative thoughts contribute significantly to anxiety and depression. Challenging these thoughts help you stay focused on what is actually happening in your life and with your family, as well as to shift to a more positive mindset. The next time you notice a negative thought pattern, challenge the accuracy of the thought. Does your belief in the thought weaken? For example, if the thought is, *my child's math teacher must think I don't care that they lose their worksheets all the time.* The challenge question may be, *What's the evidence?* Ask yourself, *Did the teacher ever say that? What is another thing that the teacher could be thinking?* The teacher could be thinking how hard it is to keep track of worksheets when your child struggles with organization. Or, the teacher could be thinking, *this parent has tried everything.* Sample challenge questions include:

- What is the evidence that this is true?
- Is there another explanation?
- What is another possible outcome?
- What is the worst-case scenario here? If that were to come true, it may be uncomfortable, but can I manage?
- Is thinking this way helpful?
- Am I questioning my worth as a person because of one thing that has happened?
- Am I trying to predict the future?

89

• Am I expecting more of myself than I would of others?

• Am I only noticing the negative side of things?

• Am I thinking "all or nothing" thoughts?

The easiest way to gain insight into your habitual ways of thinking is to keep a thought log. Take note every time you feel a negative emotion (anger, sadness, guilt, shame, etc.). Try to identify the *thought* that comes with the emotion. Then, use the challenge questions. Note what happens to your belief in the thought. Does it weaken?

Tip: *Like building any other new habit, it will take time to truly believe the thought challenge. Keep practicing! Over time, your ability to believe the thought challenges and to challenge thoughts in the moment will increase.*

Below is a sample thought log. Practice tracking your thoughts throughout the day for a few weeks.

Event	Emotion	Thought	Challenge Question	Challenge Response
Example: Bad feedback at work	Rejected, embarrassed, shameful	I am a failure	Am I questioning my worth as a person because of one thing that has happened?	Yes. There are plenty of examples of tasks at work that I have done well on. This is one task. It does not define my entire career.
Example: My child had a temper tantrum after I told them it was time to leave the playground.	Frustrated. Embarrassed	The other parents think I am a bad parent.	What is the evidence that this is true? What is something else they could be thinking?	I don't have any evidence that the parents think this, as no one has told me or led me to believe that they think I am a bad parent. They also could have been thinking, *It's not just my kid that acts this way.*

91

Event	Emotion	Thought	Challenge Question	Challenge Response

Event	Emotion	Thought	Challenge Question	Challenge Response

Event	Emotion	Thought	Challenge Question	Challenge Response

Event	Emotion	Thought	Challenge Question	Challenge Response

95

Letting Go Meditation

The last step is to practice *letting go* of the negative thoughts. This skill incorporates many of the mindfulness elements we've discussed so far, including being aware of our thoughts, taking a mindful pause, incorporating deep breathing, not reacting, and doing so without judgement Most meditations on letting go typically include a visualization, where you picture letting go of the negative thought or feeling.

- Get into a comfortable position, either seated or laying down. Put your focus inward by closing your eyes and breathing deeply from the diaphragm. Visualize the tension and stress leaving your body with each exhale.

- After several exhales, start to imagine yourself sitting in a grassy field. Visualize yourself using mindfulness techniques to describe the scene: *What do you see? What do you hear? What do you smell? What do you feel?*

- Imagine the feel of the warm sun. Imagine the sound of a bird singing in the distance, the feel of the grass under your feet, and the smell of the fresh flowers.

- Once you have created the scene, imagine looking up at the sky. Imagine each negative thought as a cloud passing by. Watch the cloud as it floats peacefully across the sky.

Do not engage further with the thought. You are not trying to change it or work through it. You are just observing it. Watch any additional thoughts that arise also float across the sky.

Continue breathing in and out while you watch your thoughts drift like clouds.

You Can Do This!

Within this workbook, there is a lot to know, learn, and practice. You are probably feeling overwhelmed right now – this is normal!

Acknowledge how you are feeling! But don't forget to also recognize how hard you are working to better yourself and your family.

Let's take a moment to focus on self-compassion and peace through a self-love and kindness meditation before you continue on your learning journey.

Buddha once said, *Unless we treat ourselves with love and compassion, we cannot reflect the same on others*. If we want to be able to be patient and kind with our loved ones, we have to practice those qualities first on ourselves. Isn't that exactly what we need right now when we're feeling overwhelmed with these new tasks, this new language and this new way of thinking and feeling?

The benefits of a self-love and kindness meditation include increased self-appreciation, gratitude, and encouragement. Research suggests this has positive effects on our emotional and physical well-being, leaving us feeling peaceful and empowered.

Start this meditation as you would any other: get comfortable in your seat and take a few deep breaths. Pair your deep breathing with empowering, self-compassionate affirmations.

Here is one I like:

May I be peaceful
May I find strength
May I be happy

Key Takeaways

This chapter discussed specific approaches to calm parenting in the midst of chaos. We focused on affirmations, proper deep breathing techniques and a Progressive Muscle Relaxation. We learned skills to help build awareness around our emotions and thoughts, including the ACA Method and negative thought challenges.

- A mindful pause helps the nervous system regroup and find balance. This allows us to *respond* instead of *reacting* in a stressful situation.
- Progressive Muscle Relaxations help to better manage the physical effects of stress.
- The ACA model can be used as a way of identifying or acknowledging negative emotions, finding what is within our control in a given situation, and accepting our reality.
- We must *acknowledge* negative emotions, identify what is *controllable* in an uncontrollable situation and *accept* the experience of negative emotions.
- Thought challenging helps us to consider alternative perspectives to our negative thoughts.

Chapter 5:
Parenting Positively

You may have heard the term *positive parenting* or even *gentle parenting*. These new buzz words are actually referring to a parenting style know as *authoritative parenting*. This term was originally coined in 1968 by psychologist Diane Baumrind. She found that this type of parent made reasonable demands on their children and provided explanations for their expectations and rules. Therefore, while parents exert high authority over their children, they do so in a manner that is warm, affectionate and respectable. Children raised in this way have been found to have the best outcomes in terms of being mentally healthy, as well as self-reliant and achievement oriented. This chapter will introduce strategies that will help you utilize your mindfulness skills to parent positively.

Before we get started, keep in mind that some of our go-to parenting strategies (modeled by our own parents), may be outdated, ineffective or simply wrong. In the book, *Children Are From Heaven,* Dr John Gray states that there are 5 important messages that our children need to hear:

- It's OK to be different
- It's OK to make mistakes
- It's OK to express negative emotions

- It's OK to want more

- It's OK to say no, but remember, mom and dad are the bosses

Remember our earlier points about *acknowledging* and *accepting* thoughts and emotions; it's important that we acknowledge and accept our children, including their thoughts, desires, fears, quirks, and differences. Our goal here is to parent the children we *have,* not the children we *want.*

By conveying these messages, even while parenting through chaos, we are doing so with mutual respect and understanding, and letting our children know they are loved, supported and accepted.

Case Study

Tali is the mother of 4-year-old June. June struggles with transitions and following directions. June gets in trouble often at preschool because she does not like to end one activity to go to the next. Her teachers have started giving her 3 minute and 1-minute warnings that an activity is going to end, but June still refuses to move on, and often acts out when the teachers try to help her clean up. At home, her behavior is worst. When Tali tells her it's time to turn off the TV and get ready for bed, she throws herself on the floor and has a tantrum. Once, when Tali told her she had to put her crayons away so that they could go to Grandma's, June got so angry she started coloring on the walls. Tali enrolled in a positive parenting program to learn how to work better with June. Tali learned key principles such as offering praise and reinforcing the opposite of the problem behavior. Tali and June collaborated to create a reward chart to help June work towards having easier transitions from playtime to bedtime. June was rewarded for behaviors such as acknowledging that she received a transition warning, putting her toys away, changing into her pajamas, picking out a bedtime story, and saying goodnight to Charlie, her teddy bear (this one was June's pick!).

Affirmation

These are the moments my child needs me most

Which Parenting Style Are You?

Let's take a moment to understand what the different types of parenting styles are. The way parents interact with their children has a direct influence on them and different parenting styles are associated with different outcomes in behavior.

The table below outlines the 4 main parenting styles, and the outcomes each has on children's personality and subsequent behaviors.

Parenting Style	Key Features	Effects on Child's Personality and Behaviors:
Authoritarian *It's my way or the highway*	You have total control and you make the rules.	Anxious
	Guide children's behavior through punishment	Aggressive
	Dismiss your child's thoughts and feelings	Low self-esteem
Authoritative *Balanced*	Explain the reasoning behind the rules you make and why they should be obeyed	Confident
	Explain the consequences of your child's behavior	Cooperative
	Empower your child's decision making	Self-reliant

Permissive *Easy-going*	Affectionate and want to please your child	Little self-reliance
	Lack of limits and consequences	Demanding
	Easily manipulated and have a hard time saying no	Lack of self-control
Uninvolved *Disengaged*	Emotionally removed from child	Depression
	No discipline	Anxiety
	Inconsistent parenting	Behavior problems

Take a few moments to reflect on the key features of each style. Being honest with yourself, which category of parenting describes you? Which behaviors and disciplinary tactics do you use that are consistent with this parenting style?

_____

_____

_____

Daily Parenting Review

As with most of the skills that you've learned so far, understanding where you currently are will help identify strengths, weaknesses, trends and areas for improvement. Since we cannot objectively observe ourselves, it is important to track our parenting habits. Use the worksheet to track your daily parenting habits for the next week.

Today I felt:

	Sun	Mon	Tue	Wed	Thu	Fri	Sat
Overwhelmed							
Exhausted							
Positive							
Pessimistic							
Anxious							

Joyful							
Energetic							
Frustrated							
Burned out							
Optimistic							
Other:							

You also want to have an honest review of your actions during challenging parenting moments. For the next week, take time to reflect each day on your child's behavior, particularly when they weren't listening, did not following directions etc. Use the chart below to track how you responded in each moment.

Today, when my child did not listen, I:

Circle yes or no for each behavior

Yes / **No**	Listened attentively
Yes / **No**	Provided a consequence in a calm manner.
Yes / **No**	Took a chance to connect with my child, even for five minutes.
Yes / **No**	Provided structure by setting expectations for them.
Yes / **No**	Let them decide how much they wanted to participate in their responsibilities, without consequence.

(Quick note: Your goal is to eventually be able to answer yes to each of these).

The best part of today as a parent was:

_____

This is the worst thing I did as a parent today:

_____

I would rate my parenting today as (1 = worst, 10 = best):

_____

Weekly Parenting Reflection

At the end of the week, answer the following questions to help reflect on your overall parenting habits.

1. As you look back over your parenting logs from this week, what do you notice?

_____

_____

2. How was your overall mood and health this week?

_____

_____

3. How was your self-care?

_____

_____

4. What did you learn from your worst-rated day of parenting?

_____

_____

5. What did you learn from your best-rated day of parenting?

_____

_____

6. How can you carry that into next week?

_____

_____

Quality Time with Your Child

The goal of quality playtime is to engage in 5 minutes *every day* of special playtime with your child. This type of special playtime is wonderful quality time that you can create with your child of any age. Create a routine of spending 5 minutes every day engaging in play of your child's choice. This can be legos or dolls for smaller kids. Finger-nail painting, model car sets or non-violent video games are appropriate for older kids, but note that the length of special playtime may have to be extended.

This playtime is special because you will make a deliberate effort to allow your child to take the lead in play. You should show excitement to join in and focus on their good behavior.

It's important that during this time you:

- Ask questions (such as What are you making now? What does this do?) as these can be frustrating or can make the child feel like they are failing if the answer is incorrect.
- Imitate your child: This is an excellent opportunity for your child to take control. Imitate the way your child is playing, such as building blocks the same way. This shows that you are paying attention, but also is incredibly validating to the child. The behaviors that you imitate are likely to be repeated.

- Mindfully sportscast: Much like your favorite game-day sportscaster, describe out loud, what your child is doing. You're drawing with the green crayon. *You're building with the yellow blocks. You're putting the sparkly shoes on the doll.* This type of running commentary has several benefits, including letting the child know that they still have your full attention, as well as that you are interested in what they are doing.
- Offer praise frequently: According to parenting specialists, during this type of special play, parents should offer praise ***every 30 seconds.*** Aim for praise that is specific, wonderful coloring! *Great job sharing!* Not only does this type of reinforcement encourage your child to repeat the praised behaviors, it also will make them feel good, thereby increasing their self-esteem!

It is important that during this time you do not:

- Criticize their efforts or any behaviors and instead, ignore minor inappropriate behaviors (only comment if the behavior is dangerous)
- Direct the way they play (avoid words such as *No, Don't, Stop*)
- Give commands (such as *Look at this, Put this there* etc.)

Note that several of the components in special playtime work because they are encouraging your child to repeat a behavior that you are praising. This is idea behind positive reinforcement: we tend to repeat behaviors that have been responded to in a positive way. Consider this: if you tell a joke at a party and everyone laughs, you are much more likely to repeat the same joke in another social situation. If no one laughed at your joke, what is the likelihood that you would tell it again? This principle is an effective strategy at helping to change behavior.

Use the chart below to track your progress:

	Sun	Mon	Tues	Wed	Thurs	Fri	Sat
Had 5 minutes of special play time							
Child and activity:							
Notes:							

Strategic Attention

As parents, we often think correcting behavior and punishment is important for stopping and modifying behavior: but research shows that punishment is not always effective. Punishment sometimes *increases* the frequency of an undesired behavior, simply because it becomes attention-seeking. Punishment does not *teach* children what to do. Often, the only lesson that comes with a punishment is the onset of negative emotions or self-believes, children may feel shameful or guilty, or start to internalize that they are "bad." Punishment can also cause children to become angry or resentful of parents for taking away a privilege. There certainly is a place for punishment, but let's first focus on the strategies that you should be implementing.

The first step is to identify the behaviors that you would like to change. The goal here then, is to use the same strategies from your special time together to reinforce the *opposite* behavior. For example, if your child is loud and rude when in public spaces, the behaviors you would *want to increase* might be talking quietly and saying please and thank you. Your job then would be to be on the lookout for your child performing these behaviors, and to use specific praise and sports casting. *I like how quietly you are playing with your trucks. You did such a good job remembering to say thank you.* At the same time, when your child raises their voice or is rude, you will not comment or respond to those behaviors.

Use the table below to track your child's behavior and your praise for the opposite behavior.

Negative Behavior:	Positive Opposite Behavior:	Offered Praise:						
		Sunday	Monday	Tuesday	Wednesday	Thursday	Friday	Saturday

Using the I-message

Communication is a key component of authoritative parenting, as many of the components depend on a parent's ability to effectively communicate with their child. It is important that communication is responsive and open. Rules and expectations are explained, with a rationale for the rules provided. Negative behaviors and consequences are discussed ahead of time.

I-Statements are an effective tool for communicating during chaos. This approach helps to clearly communicate concerns, feelings and needs without escalating the conflict. These statements allow for an open dialogue to occur, instead of the other individual feeling threatened, blamed, accused or attacked. I-Statements are easy, and are composed of:

> "I" + your feelings, needs or thoughts + the reason for your feeling, desire or thought.

I feel ... when ... because

This approach avoids using "you" statements, since they can be perceived as threatening, and cause the other person to become defensive. *You don't listen to me when I tell you things!*

Examples

Instead of:	*Say:*
Stop throwing sand!	I feel worried when you throw sand because it might get into the other children's eyes.
How many times do I have to tell you not to touch the hot stove!	I feel worried when you touch the stove that you might burn your hand.

Your turn. Write an I-message for each scenario.

You always miss your curfew and come home late.

_____

You have no right to say that to me!

_____

You should know better.

_____

You did it again? We talked about this!

_____

TIP: Talking to Older Children

As children grow, it is common that pleasant conversations begin happening less and less, particularly in families where there is a lot of chaos. Good communication is vital to parent-child bonding. It is imperative that communication is not limited to ensuring that your children did their chores and correcting them when they do something wrong. Use the list below to help engage in meaningful conversations with your older children. Place a check next to each item that you have tried.

	Pay attention and eliminate distractions
	Offer praise
	Ask open-ended questions about their hobbies and interests
	Be open and approachable. You *want* your children to come to you when they are having a problem.
	Expect that they will make bad decisions. Remember that making poor choices and wrong decisions – within reason – is often age-appropriate. Don't pass judgment or react. Instead, be a support and validate their feelings. *I'm so sorry that happened to you. What can you do now?*
	Don't problem solve unless they ask you to.

Ways to Keep the Conversation Going:

• Avoid yes / no questions that can halt a conversation
• Instead:
• Tell me more
• How so?
• Do you want to talk about it?
• What was that like?

What Is Rewarding to Your Child?

Thus far, we've discussed rewarding behaviors that we would like to see continue through praise, which is a social reward. Other social rewards include giving affection, a smile, a warm tap on the arm or a high-five. Other types of rewards include privileges, such as TV / videogame time, later bedtime, special time with friends), or material rewards such as money, snacks and toys.

Rewards are in the eye of the beholder, so make sure you are enticing your children with things that they find rewarding. Fill out the table below with some ideas of rewards. Enlist the help of your child!

Social Rewards	Privileges	Material Rewards

Tip: Reward consistently, and only if the goal has been met. Make sure you offer praise and a smile when giving the reward – the social reward is an added bonus! Once your child is earning rewards consistently, switch to sporadic rewards.

"To a child, love is spelled T-I-M-E."

-Zig Ziglar

If you are reading this book, we already can assume that a significant portion of your family life is spent in chaos or conflict. Making sure that you are still making time for positive interactions with your children is vital to overall relationship health.

Children are motivated by their parent's attention and will alter their behavior to seek it. This includes negative behaviors and acting out. Therefore, one way to eliminate attention-seeking negative behaviors, to increase your child's self-esteem and to strengthen your relationship is by engaging to *special playtime* daily with your child. This is intentional, individual, distraction (and phone) free quality time with your child.

Take a few moments to reflect on how much time you typically spend with your child. Is it enough?

Key Takeaways

This chapter introduced the idea of authoritative parenting, and refers to the type of parent who makes reasonable demands on their children and provides explanations for their expectations and rules. These children have been found to have the best outcomes. Strategies were introduced to help utilize mindfulness skills to parent positively. Acknowledging, accepting and parenting the children we *have* not the children we *want* is vital to letting our children know that they are loved, supported and accepted.

In this chapter, we:

- Identified our parenting style
- Tracked and reflected on our parenting habits
- Engaged in special playtime with our children where we practiced key parenting skills
- Implemented strategic attention
- Practiced using I- messages
- Implemented rewards for our children's behavior

Chapter 6:
Active Listening

Improving communication and listening skills is an important step for strengthening and empowering any relationship, especially those between parents and their children. This chapter will explore the fundamentals of active listening, breaking down the components of this communication style and incorporating mindfulness techniques to encourage your child to share and open up. We will explore how actively listening to your child can help create a safe, secure environment in which your child feels comfortable expressing themselves. By understanding the importance of active listening and its components, you can better equip yourself to build a strong, meaningful relationship with your child.

As parents, we always act in the best interest of our children. You want to foster good values and goals in our child while discouraging undesirable behaviors. However, remember that children, from a young age, are independent thinkers and feelers. In other words, there is a reason and a motivation behind their choices.

Active listening skills provide you the opportunity to *learn* why your child acts the way they do rather than making *assumptions* about why they behave the way they do. You probably will not agree with their choices. As an adult with life experience and fully developed problem-solving capabilities, you aren't supposed to. However, having a better grasp of your child's thought process and emotional experience will allow you to intervene and educate your child in a more effective manner, frequently in conjunction with your child.

Case Study

Charlie was seething with anger as he angrily slammed the front door and kicked off his cleats in the living room. His baseball practice had not gone well, and his frustration was evident in his every move. He threw his bat bag against the wall with a loud thud before angrily stomping up the stairs. His face was twisted in a scowl as he continued to his bedroom, where he slammed the door shut behind him. Charlie was clearly in no mood to be reasoned with, and it seemed he would not be calmed down any time soon.

If this had occurred a few weeks earlier, Charlie's mother, Jolie, would have chased him up the stairs and yelled at him about his disrespect for her house. Jolie, however, has been honing her skills as an active listener, so instead of getting upset, she went calmly upstairs to Charlie's room.

Jolie knocked on the bedroom door rather than immediately scolding him for slamming the door and throwing his ball bag and cleats, as she had done many times in the past. While standing in his doorway, she said, "Can you tell me what happened?"

Charlie explained that Lon, the team's star player, was not allowed to participate in today's game since he skipped practice earlier in the week so that he and his brother could go see a movie. Charlie stated that the game was important because it was against a rival school, who was their largest opponent. Charlie's Coach would not make an exception to the rule, despite the fact that the squad desperately needed Lon. The score remained tied until the bottom of the ninth inning when the opposing school broke the tie with a series of consecutive runs scored. Jolie said, "It sounded like you were disappointed that Coach wouldn't allow Lon to play. That does sound disappointing. You must be so angry with Coach, and for losing the game."

Reflect on how the conversation may have gone without Jolie using active listening skills while talking to Charlie.

1. What do you think the outcome of the conversation would have been if instead, Jolie had yelled about Charlie slamming doors and leaving his cleats in the living room?

_____

_____

2. Charlie said that the team lost because Coach wouldn't make an exception to let Lon play. How do you think Charlie would

have reacted if Jolie said that Lon wasn't allowed to play as a consequence of his own actions?

_____

_____

Affirmation

In this moment, I am present.

"The majority of individuals do not listen with the intention of comprehending what is being said; rather, they listen with the intention of responding."

— Stephen R. R. Covey

Active listening is a great tool to help improve communication with others. Children have a greater sense of connection, understanding, and support when their parents actively listen to them. This ability to listen leads to opportunities for parents to help children explore, clarify, and learn about appropriate methods to express their thoughts, feelings and behaviors.

Active Listening Reflection

In Chapter 2, we discussed the Empty Hands Listening technique, in which you give your child your undivided attention while they are speaking and, more importantly, do so with empty hands. Being completely present is a core component of active listening. Additional principals of active listening include:

- Maintaining eye contact with the speaker.
- Maintaining open, inviting body language.
- Paying attention to nonverbal behaviors, such as tone, facial cues, and body language.
- Not interjecting, even if that results in a few seconds of silence.
- Refraining from mentally formulating a response or solution.
- Refraining from passing judgment on the behavior, opinions, or feelings of the person who is speaking.
- Keep an open mind, even your perspective is different.
- Clarify understanding and keep the conversation moving forward by asking questions.
- Avoid yes/no questions by using open-ended statements that help continue the conversation, such as *How did you feel about that? What are your thoughts on the matter? Tell me more...*
- Paraphrase and reflect. *It sounds like you're saying... What happened next? That sounds really difficult.*
- Lastly, don't try to problem solve! Your role – no matter who the speaker is – is to listen and support.

Consider the most recent interaction you had with your child when your child was talking, did you:

	YES	NO
Stop what you were doing.		
Maintain eye contact?		
Maintain open and inviting body language.		
Interrupt when your child was talking?		
Offer solutions to their problems?		
Ask questions to clarify understanding.		
Mentally prepare a solution?		
Allow space for your child to revisit the conversation.		

It is not possible to actively listen while engaging in items 4, 5, or 7. Keep in mind that finding solutions to problems is not the point of practicing active listening. Your child does not always need answers, but does always need to be heard, understood and supported.

Think about who you go to when you are having a difficult time. Maybe it's a partner, friend or family member. When you confide in that person, what do they do that makes you feel seen, heard and supported?

_____

_____

_____

Take a moment to reflect on your results in the previous exercise. Are you surprised by the outcome? Use the lines below for your notes.

_____

_____

_____

_____

As we move forward, it is important to keep in mind that the majority of people who are good listeners are also good at *reflecting*, which means they are able to repeat what the speaker has just said, but they do so in their own words. Not only does this demonstrate that you were paying attention, but it also conveys support and empathy. When working on this with your child, keep in mind that the tone you use is important. Maintain a casual tone and a conversational stance. Even if your child is unable to verbalize their feelings, it is important to observe their body language and facial expressions for clues as to what they are experiencing.

Reflective Listening Formula

The table below presents an easy tool to use to construct reflective statements. Can you think of any additional statements that may be helpful when practicing reflective listening?

Opener	+ Emotion	+ About / Because / When + Thought
It sounds like	You feel sad	About
If I hear you correctly	You feel hurt	Because of
I'm not sure I follow	You feel embarrassed	When
You seem to be saying	You feel frustrated	About
I get a sense that	You feel angry	Because of
Let me make sure I understand	You feel angry	When

Practicing Reflective Listening

Below is a list of samples statements made by younger children. Read each statement and consider the possible emotion each child may be experiencing. Compose a response using reflective listening that demonstrates that you comprehend their feelings.

Child's Statement	Emotion	Parent's Response
Patrice said, *I wanted to run for a position on the student council; but no one would vote for me*.		
Jax said, *Mr. Fines is such a bully. Today he forced me to stay inside and fix my homework instead of going to recess.*		
Rava said, *I hate you! You don't let me do anything!*		

127

Shauna said, I *don't understand why I have to do this math homework, it's pointless!*		
Shauna said, I *don't understand why I have to do this math homework, it's pointless!*		
Eduardo said, *I'd like to punch Pal in the face*!		

"Silence is sometimes the best answer."

- Dalai Lama

Getting Comfortable with Silence

Being comfortable with a few moments of silence is a cornerstone of being a good listener, but it is also something that most people struggle with. It seems counterintuitive, given that we talk about improving communication and listening through techniques

128

such as I-statements and reflective listening that encourage speaking, however, silence may be incredibly beneficial. Our natural inclination is to avoid "awkward silence," as research shows that a continuous conversation flow creates a sense of social validation, and belongingness in a group setting.

Nevertheless, "sitting in silence" is a method that therapists use that frequently gives patients the opportunity to pause and think about their experiences. It frequently conveys the therapist's feelings of support and empathy to the patient. Instead of rushing to fill the gaps in conversation with your child (or anyone else, for that matter), try to take a mindful pause and give the speaker a moment to continue processing, reflecting, and collecting their thoughts. You can do this by not rushing to fill the gaps in conversation with your child (or anyone else, for that matter). This moment of silence often leads to a deeper connection as well as more meaning conversation.

This is a great opportunity to practice mindful pause skills. With a child, partner or friend, take turns sharing about something that is bothering you right now or that you are struggling with. Practice your active listening abilities while the speaker is talking. Allow for breaks in the flow of the conversation, and time for reflection and processing by practicing the mindful pause. Give the speaker comfortable space before responding.

Sitting in Silence Reflection

Reflect on how challenging sitting in a moment of silence is. Consider how difficult it is to be silent for a moment during conversation.

_____

_____

_____

During the period of silence, what thoughts and feelings did you find yourself having?

_____

_____

_____

How difficult was it to create and maintain a moment of silence? What happened to the conversation following the moment of silence?

_____

_____

_____

Active Listening Checklist

You have now learned the fundamentals of active listening. Let's put everything together! Use the checklist below to help remember all of the components of active listening.

Show You Are Listening:

Question	YES	NO
Have you removed all potential sources of distraction?		
Did you communicate verbally, for example, by saying things like *hh hmm*, *I understand*, or *that makes sense?*		
Did you use nonverbal communication, such as smiling, maintaining eye contact, and head nodding?		

Show You Are Interested:

Question	YES	NO
Did you ask open-ended questions for clarification, such as *What was that like?* or, *what were you thinking in that moment?*		

Did you try to keep the conversation going by asking open-ended questions such as or, *what happened next" What do you think you should do from here?*		
Did you paraphrase and reflect? *That sounds stressful!*		

Remember to:

- Maintain eye contact
- Maintain good body language
- Avoid problem-solving
- Keep an open mind
- Be comfortable with silence

ABCs of Behavior

While active listening can help improve communication and understanding, what happen when our children are not talking? We need tools to help interpret behaviors as well. Understanding *why* a child is engaging in a negative behavior can help guide parental interventions. Think of behavior as a means of nonverbal communication. Here is an easy example: Your child routinely acts out when you tell them it is time to go to the doctor. Why? They don't want to go to the doctor because the last time they got a shot and it was painful. Instead of saying, *I'm afraid of having to get another shot,* they act out by refusing to get in the car.

The ABC Method can help us translate children's behavior.

A is the antecedent: What happened before the behavior?

B is the behavior: What did the child say or do? How severe was it? How long did it last?

C is the consequence: What happens after the behavior, that may make the behavior more or less likely to occur again?

Tracking the ABC's of your child's behaviors can give insight into common triggers, or antecedents, of why they are engaging in those behaviors. Are they acting out of hunger? Anxiety? Fear? Think of the consequences – or what does the child get out of this behavior? Sometimes, the consequence *encourages* the behavior. This is the case with avoidance or attention (even negative attention can be reinforcing!) Remember, the specific reason for a behavior may not be clear every single time. Track consistently so that you can pick up on trends in your child's behavior.

Examples of ABCs

Antecedent	Behavior	Consequence
Asked to work on a task	Crying	Verbally corrected
Asked to perform a chore	Screaming / yelling	Removed from class / situation
Transitioning between activities	Hitting peer / sibling / adult	Work or goal-directed behavior changed

Exercise

Take a moment to reflect on your child's behavior. What ABC's can you identify?

Antecedent	Behavior	Consequence
Math teacher gives out a worksheet to do in class.	Max says he won't do it, crumples it up, and throws it in the trashcan.	Max is sent to the principal's office, missing the rest of math class.

Continue tracking ABC's. What trends emerge?

_____

_____

_____

_____

_____

_____

In chapter 1, I quoted a statistic that 87 percent of children who were diagnosed with ADHD were found to have coexisting disorder, most frequently an emotional disorder. Children do not always have the cognitive skills or language required to articulate their emotional distress. They might not be aware that what they

Don't Forget to Consider Emotional Reasons for Behavior

are feeling is actually anxiety or embarrassment, but the physical symptoms of these emotions are driving their behaviors This is why active listening and ABC skills are so important: you may need to translate, and then educate, your child on identifying, labeling and working through these important emotions.

Consider this example about anxiety. As adults who have learned about emotions, we are able to say, *I'm worried about this presentation… I'm scared to hear the doctor's feedback…I'm nervous about what happens next.*

Note that these are skills that must be taught and practiced, and are not just age-dependent. There are plenty of adults that struggle to talk about and process their emotions. Unspoken anxiety in children may look like:

• Difficulty falling or stating asleep
• Feeling agitated or angry
• Defiance
• Challenging behaviors
• Avoiding school, activities or events
• Physical symptoms such as headaches or stomachaches
• Trying to control people or events
• Having expectations of themselves or others
• Problems with attention or focus

Keep in mind that problematic behaviors may be masking underlying emotional distress. Anxiety, sadness, embarrassment, fear, shame, nervousness, self-doubt, or envy are some of the emotions that could fall into this category.

Key Takeaways

Children are able to feel connected, understood, and supported when active listening is practiced, making it an excellent tool for improving communication with other people. The primary aspects of attentive listening were the emphasis of this chapter's discussion. Among the most important takeaways are:

- Use Empty Hands Listening when active listening.
- With active listening, maintain eye contact and open body language.
- With active listening, do not interrupt or problem solve.
- Apply the formula for reflective listening: Opener + Emotion + About / Because / When + Thought
- Offer space when listening, and practice getting comfortable with silence.
- Focus on the ABC's to help understand your child's behavior.
- Consider underlying emotional symptoms as additional explanation for behavior.

PART III:

Practicing Mindfulness Skills for ADHD with Your Child

Chapter 7:

Developing Shared Goals and Expectations

Introduction

Goal-setting is a valuable skill that is beneficial throughout the lifespan. Setting goals gives us a path forward and can help to motivate us to put in the effort to achieve. Achieving milestones along the way to the goal is a boost to our self-esteem. Teaching our children how to set and work towards goals can help them understand their own strengths and weaknesses, provide opportunities for success, and teach essential lessons in prioritization, planning, and decision-making. When your child sets their own goals (with a little support from parents), they become intrinsically motivated to achieve them. They accept responsibility for it and are much more likely to meet it. The act of creating goals together can also provide a chance for parent and child connection.

Remember to keep in mind the 6Cs of goal setting that were introduced in Chapter 2:

- Conversation: Discuss goals and the parent's expectations with the child, giving them a chance to offer suggestions.
- Collaboration: The parent and child should work together to develop goals.
- Clarity and Consistency: Your child's goals should be specific and consistent, as well as attainable for their age and skills.
- Choices: Give your child options so that they feel included in the process.
- Check-In: Check in with them along the way, offering support and discussing the process and their progress.

Case Study

Asher is in the fifth grade. Getting to school on time is difficult for him because of his diagnosis of ADHD. He frequently can't find his school bag, has to hurry upstairs for a file or notebook, and occasionally remembers he forgot his lunch after he is already outside. When Asher is late for school, he misses the morning assembly. This is significant because the Principal has begun to distribute school spirit items such as fancy pens, pencils, pins, and keychains with the school name and colors, and Asher has never been there to get any. Asher discussed with his father the importance of arriving to school on time, and they agreed to set a goal of getting to school on time one day per week to begin. To attain this goal, Asher will prepare for the morning by doing two things before going to bed:

packing his schoolbag and leaving it by the front door. On days that Asher arrives at school on time, he will be rewarded by being able to choose the TV show that he and his brother watch while Dad makes dinner. Asher struggled at first to properly pack his schoolbag, so he and his father modified the goal. They developed a checklist for Asher's schoolbag: after doing his schoolwork, he had to ensure he put his homework folder, notebook, and pencil case back in his school bag. Asher's father created a colorful checklist, which they keep next to the desk where Asher works. Asher doesn't always do it right, but most nights, he gets all three items inside his school bag. They'll modify the goal whenever Asher gets better at organizing his schoolbag.

Affirmation

With every exhale, I get one step closer to achieving my goals.

The activities below will help you identify areas for improvement.

Shared Journaling

For the Parent:

In the space below, journal about the relationship you have with your child. What do you enjoy most about your relationship? What would you like to have more of? How do you believe your relationship can be strengthened?

_____

_____

_____

_____

_____

For the Child:

In the space below, journal about your relationship with your parent. What do you like most about your relationship? What would you like to have more of? How do you believe your relationship can be strengthened? *(It's OK if you want your parent to write your responses for you).*

_____

_____

_____

_____

_____

When you are finished, share your responses with one another.

If you are completing this workbook with younger children, modify any exercise by taking turns drawing and coloring their responses to the questions. Use your drawings as a prompt for discussion. You may also read the prompts aloud and record your child's answers.

What Are Your Goals in Each Area of Your Life?

It is important to set both short and long-term goals. Setting only long-term goals may feel unattainable and can be demotivating and discouraging. Setting smaller short-term goals helps build confidence in ourselves and keeps us on track while we work towards reaching the longer-term goals. This activity can help you identify short and long-term goals.

What are Your Short and Long-Term Goals?

Parents:

Area	Short-Term Goals	Long-Term Goals
Social		
Academic		
Career		
Health		
Athletic		
Family		
Other		

Child:

Area	Short-Term Goals	Long-Term Goals
Social		
Academic		
Career		

Health		
Athletic		
Family		
Other		

What Are Your Goals for Each Role in Your Life?

You've now considered short and long-term goals in a variety of life domains. Take a moment to pause and reflect on these ideas.

Let's take this activity a step further and identify goals for *who* you want to be. Setting these goals will help you be open and aware of your behaviors in these areas, will help you take actionable steps toward success, and will help hold you accountable for growing and evolving toward goal completion.

What Are Your Goals in Your Role?

Parent:

As a son/daughter:

_____

As a sibling/cousin:

_____

As a parent:

_____

As a spouse:

_____

As a friend:

_____

As a student:

_____

As an employee:

_____

_____

In other roles you hold:

_____

Child:

As a son/daughter:

_____

As a sibling/cousin:

_____

As a parent:

As a spouse:

_____

As a friend:

_____

As a student:

_____

As an employee:

_____

In other roles you hold:

_____

Grown Up You

It is beneficial to have conversations with your children about their dreams for the future. Remember your active listening skills! Don't judge! Instead, keep an open mind and be supportive! Make this a fun, open dialogue by sharing your own responses to the questions below.

146

1. What do you want to be when you grow up??

2. What fun activities do you want to do?

3. What does your future family look like?

4. Where do you want to travel to?

5. What accomplishments do you want to achieve?

6. What skills do you aspire to have?

7. What adventures do you dream about having?

8. What places do you want to visit?

9. What abilities do you hope to gain?

10. What would you feel proud to overcome?

11. What do you hope to learn?

12. How can I help you reach your goals?

The Magic Wand

Over the next few days, both you and your child should take some time and fantasize: Imagine a future version of yourself. Now, wave a magic wand. What have you accomplished? What has changed? What is different in each area of your life? Write your reflections on the lines below.

Parent:

1. What have you achieved?

147

2. What is different?

3. What is unique about each aspect of your life? Think about where you reside, your job, your interests, and your friends.

4. What steps do you need to take *now* to start working towards this version of yourself?

Child:

1. What have you achieved?

2. What is different?

3. What is unique about each aspect of your life? Think about where you reside, your job, your interests, and your friends.

4. What steps do you need to take *now* to start working towards this version of yourself?

Setting Goals Together - Remember To Be Mindful

When spending time reflecting on dreams, goals and visions of the future, it is not unusual to be reminded of our failures. Keep in mind that goal-setting exercises are not meant to highlight our weaknesses but instead should create motivation and encouragement for self-improvement. Let's practice keeping a positive outlook but taking a mindful pause.

We can all fall into a thinking pattern where we dismiss our accomplishments. If this becomes habitual, we begin to forget the wonderful things we are proud of. Having a few moments each day to recall our achievements can give us a confidence boost and help with motivation.

Take a minute to reflect on your recent accomplishments, both big and small, and fill out the list below. This is a great exercise for both parent and child to complete for their own achievements.

Whenever you find yourself feeling discouraged, demotivated, or overwhelmed, return to this list. It is a great reminder of the goals you have already accomplished!

Parent

_____

_____

_____

Child

_____

_____

_____

_____

Please fill in the blanks with the following;

What are 4 things you are thankful for?

Parent:

_____

_____

_____

_____

Child:

_____

_____

_____

_____

What are your 3 best memories?

Parent:

_____

_____

_____

Child:

_____

_____

_____

What are 2 things you are very proud of?

Parent:

_____

_____

Child:

_____

_____

What is a valuable lesson you've learned?

Parent:

Child: _____

Setting Goals Together

Parent and child should review their goal lists together. Discuss which goals you can help to support. Can you narrow the focus of your goals? Can you be more specific in what you hope to achieve? Can you prioritize your goals? *Remember the 6Cs: Converse, collaborate, make goals clear, consistent, offer your child choices, and check-in along the way.*

Parents: List your first 3 goals here:

• Goal 1. _____
• Goal 2. _____
• Goal 3. _____

Child: List your first 3 goals here:

• Goal 1. _____
• Goal 2. _____
• Goal 3. _____

Let's make sure we are set up for success! Recall in Chapter 3, we discussed the need to have MAMAS in mind during goal setting. Your goals should be:

- Measurable
- Attainable
- Monitored
- Adjustable
- Simple

Remember: we are working on setting goals that are *clear* and *consistent*, and we want *to check*-in on goal attainment progress.

Setting Goals Together

The final stage is to implement your goal-setting strategy. Make sure that you are tracking goals visually so that you can easily monitor progress. Celebrate reaching milestones and offer your child positive feedback and encouragement along the way. Check-in with your child about the process, and make tweaks and modifications as necessary.

Use the table below to make sure that you set a MAMAS goal.

My Goal:	Questions	Parent	Child
Measurable	How will I measure progress and success?		
Attainable	Is this realistic?		
Monitored	How will I celebrate milestones?		
Adjustable	How can I break down the goal into smaller steps?		
Simple	What needs to be done for the goal to be considered accomplished?		

Modification for Younger Children

Goal setting is an important life skill that you can start modeling for your children at an early age. Below is an exercise you can do with younger children to help them create goals.

Three Stars and A Wish

Name three things you are good at:

*1. _____

*2. _____

*3. _____

Name one thing you want to be better at:

*1. _____

Fun Fact About Goal Setting: Writing down your goals and having an accountability partner will help you achieve them!

Key Takeaways

This chapter focused on setting shared goals with our child. When setting goals, keep the 6C's in mind:

- *Converse* and *collaborate*
- Make your goals *clear* and *consistent*.
- Offer *choices*
- *Check-in* along the way
- We:
  - Set short and long-term goals for 6 main areas of our life
  - Set goals for 7 major roles in our lives

Interesting Goal-Setting Fact

Dr. Gail Matthews' landmark study at Dominican University demonstrated the benefits of goal setting and having a support person to hold us accountable.

Her study included 267 participants divided into 5 groups:

Group 1 was asked to think about goals they would like to set
Group 2 set goals but didn't make a plan for how they would meet them.
Group 3 had set goals and a set plan to achieve them.
Group 4 had set goals and a set plan and shared both with a supportive friend.
Group 5 had set goals and a set plan and shared both, along with a weekly progress report and with a supportive friend.

The results are hardly surprising. Group 5 had the best outcomes and achieved significantly more goals than the other groups. The study also discovered that groups that *wrote* out their goals accomplished more than those that did not.

- Waved a magic wand to help visualize a future version of ourselves
- Discussed conversation starters about our future
- Took a mindful pause to reflect on previous achievements
- Defined goals keeping MAMAS in mind

Chapter 8:
Staying Calm, Focused, And In Control

This chapter will focus on mindfulness elements that parents and children can do together to cultivate and hone mindfulness skills. There is not one right way to practice mindfulness. Everyone's preferences will influence the specific mindfulness technique that resonates with them. Keep in mind that different circumstances, triggers, and even days may require the use of a different mindfulness tool in order to remain calm, focused, and in control. For this reason, it is important to have a variety of skills available in your mindfulness toolbox. People need mindfulness for a variety of reasons. For some, it is to help stay calm, while others use it to help stay focused. Some of the exercises in this chapter will help you determine which areas of your life may benefit the most from mindfulness skills.

A final goal of this chapter is to discover mindfulness elements that parents and child can practice together.

Case Study

Clarissa is in fourth grade and has been diagnosed with ADHD. In class, she says she gets distracted and stops paying attention. She thinks about other things and describes her brain as going "so fast". Clarissa is often so engrossed in her daydreams that she rethinks conversations she had with her best friend, or something that happened with her parents, or something that she did in class that got her into trouble. Sometimes, Clarissa then can't pay attention because she is so upset about whatever she was thinking. Clarissa once was thinking "so hard" she missed her whole English class, which was disappointing because they read aloud from her favorite book, *Little Women.*

Clarissa has been trying to figure out how to not get so lost in her thoughts. Her grandmother drew her a STOP sign, which she colored in purple and green, her favorite colors. Clarissa keeps the stop sign taped to her desk so that when she sees it, it is a visual reminder to *STOP.* Clarissa then knows to take a moment to stop what she is doing, take a deep breath, observe what is happening both internally within her as well as externally, and to shift her focus to what she should be paying attention to.

Affirmation

There is no one better to be than myself.

Where Was Your Attention?

Have you ever finished reading something and not had any idea what you read? Have you recently been on your way somewhere, such as, in a car or on the school bus, and not remember the ride? Tell me about that time. Why do you think that happened?

_____

_____

_____

Daily Mood

Sometimes, our behavior is a direct reflection of how we are feeling. We may act out because we are feeling scared or worried, but either are not aware of how we are feeling, do not know how to convey to others how we are feeling, or do not have the skills to cope with the feeling. Most of the skills we have focused on in this workbook will help us to be more aware of those feelings and will give us tools to help us cope. Having a way to track our mood every day can help us identify patterns in our emotions and behaviors and help us to plan ahead for healthier ways to cope. As a result, you will be able to prepare for situations that might pose a challenge to you in advance, as well as be able to recover from negative emotions in a timelier manner.

For the next few days, use the tables below to keep track of your emotions and coping skills. What trends do you see?

Examples of emotions:

Happy	Sad	Excited	Worried
Frustrated	Angry	Scared	Bored
Annoyed	Impatient	Sick	Neutral

Examples of Coping Strategies

Do something else	Ask for help	Talk to my parents	Talk to a friend
Deep breaths	Take a walk	Ask for a hug	Do something creative
Listen to music	Do some stretches	Use an affirmation	Sing

Days	Today I felt	This is how I felt because	This gives my body the sensation of	This is what I did in response	Other coping strategies I can use are
Mon					
Tue					
Wed					
Thurs					
Fri					
Sat					
Sun					

Acceptance

Accepting the reality of a situation can be hard, but it can also make you feel better. In the space below, write about something that happened to you that you wish didn't. How did it make you feel? How do you feel about it now?

_____

_____

_____

Let's Tell a Story

We've spent a lot of time talking about staying in the moment. An important component of mindfulness and staying in the moment is *paying attention.* Let's see how well you can do!

Child goes first! Reach the following story aloud to your parent. When you are finished, ask your parent to retell the story using their own words. How much do they remember?

Sara Beth was walking by the river near her home. She was admiring the colors of the stones by the riverbank – blues, greens and browns. She picked up a shiny one and threw it into the water. She thought she heard a strange sound, so she stood as still as a statue and held her breath. What did she hear? Sure enough, after 6 seconds, she heard it again, a low, deep ribbit. She knew that meant that there was a frog close by. She tiptoed closer to the river, where

161

there were a bunch of yellow and white flowers. She was careful not to step on the flowers with her new red sneakers. She knelt down, picked up a small stick, and gently parted the flowers so she could peer into the water. A baby frog sat on a bright green lily pad! Hello there, Frog! Sara Beth said. The frog looked at her curiously before saying, ribbit! Suzie laughed and the frog turned and took a giant leap into the water.

Now it's your turn, parents! Read the story below aloud to your child. When you're finished, ask your child to retell the story using their own words. How much did they remember?

Pacho did well on his history test, so his uncle was giving him a treat! Pacho wanted a cupcake from the nearby bakery, so he and his uncle boarded the bus to the bakery after school. Pacho wore his favorite sweater and baseball hat for the trip. On their way, they passed the post office, the animal hospital, and the new ice cream shop. Pacho loved the smell of the cupcakes, cookies, and brownies on display in the bakery. Millie, the baker, showed Pacho her personal favorites, which included chocolate cupcakes, strawberry cupcakes, and cupcakes with pineapple chunks inside. Pacho decided on a vanilla cupcake topped with rainbow sprinkles. He also decided to get a chocolate chip cookie for his younger brother, Charlie.

Story Reflection

The previous task was designed to test your ability to *pay attention*. Identifying the reasons for your wandering attention may help you understand what you need to do to stay focused.

Think about your behaviors when you were *listening* to the story being read to you. Were you:

	Parent		Child	
Using active listening skills?	Yes	No	Yes	No
Using Empty Hands Listening?	Yes	No	Yes	No
Was it hard to stay in the moment?	Yes	No	Yes	No
Did your mind wander?	Yes	No	Yes	No
Were you distracted by any other sounds?	Yes	No	Yes	No

Several skills you have already learned in this workbook might be used here to improve your attention. Using mindful pauses before beginning a new discussion, active listening skills to communicate with the speaker, and staying present in the current moment may all be helpful.

What could you have done to have stayed present better?

Parent: _____

Child: _____

Staying in the Moment

This is something that takes practice, especially if you struggle with focus due to ADHD. Luckily, there are some simple ways to practice staying in the present. Some examples include:

Standing in the kitchen and smelling mom's fresh baked brownies

Listening to your sister practice her violin

Making eye contact with your grandmother as she tells you a story

We incorporated our senses into meditations in Chapters 2 and 3, and we can also use our senses as a way to anchor to the present moment.

Parent and child: Take turns looking around the room that you are in. Can you each describe:

- What you see
- What you hear
- What you smell
- What you taste
- What you feel

Story Meditation

Parent and child: Keeping in mind what you just learned from the story reflection, I want you to make up your own story. You can pair this exercise with deep breathing to create your own story meditation.

- Look around the room you are in.
- Create a story using as many details from the room as possible.
- Incorporate the objects, signs, colors, sounds and smells that are around you.
- Use as many details as you can.

Let's Make a STOP Sign

The case study at the beginning of this chapter depicts Clarissa using a STOP sign to help her stop daydreaming and refocus. The STOP sign meditation is a type of visualization practice. When you are feeling emotional or need to slow down, this practice encourages you to *stop* what you are doing and take a mindful pause before proceeding.

Color in the stop sign below. You will visualize this stop sign during the next meditation, so be creative! What will be the most memorable or relaxing for you? What are you most likely to pay attention to when you need to remind yourself to *stop?* You can use as many colors or patterns as you like!

Parent:

Child:

:

Stop Sign Meditation

The stop sign meditation can help you take a moment or pause. It provides us with an opportunity to adjust our emotions and behaviors from highly emotional to a more conscious response.

Sit in a comfortable position and close your eyes softly. Take a few deep breaths.

As you feel your body start to calm, visualize your stop sign. Anchor your awareness to the stop sign. If your thoughts wander, gently bring them back to your stop sign.

Now, practice STOP:

Stop what you are doing. *Press the pause button* on your thoughts and actions.

Take a few deep breaths. Focus on the sensations of your inhales and exhales.

Observe what is happening in your body and mind. What emotions do you feel? What do you feel physically? Where in your body do you feel the emotions? Visualize releasing the emotion from wherever it is held in your body with each exhale.

Proceed with whatever behavior you choose to do next, keeping in mind what you just learned.

Code Words

Family code words are a one-of-a-kind tool that parents may use to secretly remind children to be aware of their behavior.

Code words can be used as reminders:

- About behaviors that can start off as fun but turn into something that is not fun or even harmful, such as play fighting that can quickly turn too rough or not remaining seated while at a restaurant.
- To help manage emotions, such as to find calm in a moment of anxiety or when triggered to be angry.
- To refocus attention on the task at hand.

Example:

For example, a parent shouts *jumping jellyfish* when their child appears hyperactive. The child hears this and knows that they should freeze and take three deep breaths. Parents and children should answer these questions together:

1. What behavior would a code word help you to manage?

_____

2. What is a fun code word? Use your imagination and be creative!

_____

3. When you hear this code word, what will you do?

_____

Kids' Korner

This workbook has focused a lot on the parents; this sidebar is simply for the kids.

So, kids: Between you and I, mindfulness is actually a pretty cool and powerful skill. It's simple to do and it can help you in a lot of ways. Just practicing a little each day can help you calm down, be less worried, less angry, focus more, be less energetic – the list goes on and on!

As you work through this book, you will learn some strategies that will help you practice and use mindfulness every day, but I wanted to share a secret with you. There are some really *fun* ways to practice mindfulness. Keep in mind: the point of mindfulness is to take a *pause*, to be present at the moment that you are in. Something that may include paying really good attention, being observant or managing impulsiveness. Some fun mindfulness games and activities are:

- Blowing bubbles
- Blowing pinwheels
- Blowing up balloons
- Drawing
- Coloring
- Playing I Spy
- Playing Simon Says
- Playing Freeze Dance
- Playing Red Light, Green Light

Key Takeaways

The goals of this chapter included identifying fundamental areas where mindfulness may help, as well as different ways to practice mindfulness that parent and child can practice together.

Key takeaways include:

- A Story Meditation: Create a story out of the objects, signs, colors, sounds, and smells that are around you.
- The STOP sign meditation includes visualizing a stop sign to remind you to stop what you're doing and take a mindful pause before proceeding.
- Creating family code words that parents can use to secretly remind children to regulate their behavior.
- Blowing bubbles, painting, or playing Freeze Dance are some enjoyable mindfulness exercises for children.

Chapter 9:
Improving Executive Functioning Skills

Introduction

In Chapter 1, we discussed what executive function impairments might look like in children with ADHD. While each person's presentation is unique, typical challenges include *activation, focus, effort, emotion, memory,* and *action.* The purpose of this chapter is to provide tools for parents and children to identify areas of weakness, as well as routines and exercises to assist in concentrating on and improving these functional areas. Parents are advised to model behaviors that indicate some of the primary components of good executive function outside of this workbook, such as controlling their own emotions and conduct, waiting their time, controlling urges, following directions, and executing multistep orders. Simple games like *Simon Says, Red Light, Green Light,* and *Jenga* are great ways to supplement workbook exercises.

Case Study

Chi is in seventh grade and suffers from ADHD. Chi would complete the checklist his counselor helped him create whenever he was handed in-class work: feet flat on the ground, sit up properly, work flat on his desk, pen in hand, 3 deep breaths, and the affirmation, *I got this!* Despite this checklist, Chi would work for a few moments before becoming sidetracked. Last week in science class, Chi leaned back in his chair to view the class fish, and fell over, bringing his notebook with him, bruising his elbow, and losing his pencil. Chi was redirected by his teacher, but a few moments later, he was distracted by the school bus picking up 5th grade students for a field trip. This cycle of paying attention and becoming distracted is typical of Chi's day.

Chi worked closely with the guidance counselor to figure out ways to improve his attention and reduce distractibility. They began by moving his seat to the front of the class, closer to the teacher's desk, where there would be fewer distractions and where the teacher could redirect him. The counselor also conducted an experiment with him during which they discovered that the average length of his attention span was 8 minutes. Chi now keeps a stopwatch on his desk and works for 8 minutes before taking a 2-minute break. Chi lifts his hands up high and stretches throughout every 2-minute break, maintaining quiet so as not to bother his peers. Chi and his counselor are working together to increase his attention span to 10 minutes.

The Relationship between Affirmations and Executive Function

Affirmation

Everything I need is already within me.

Throughout this workbook, I have been highlighting self-affirmations as a way to ground and center ourselves and to help challenge negative thinking. I would like to highlight an additional benefit of affirmations, in the hopes that it will encourage you to stress their significance and participate in the practice with your children.

Research has found that affirmations have been linked to improved performance in both executive function and performance under stress. The Journal of Experimental Social Psychology discovered that when people use self-affirmations, they are better able to utilize executive function resources. This study discovered that individuals who used self-affirmations performed better in the areas of working memory and inhibition than those who did not use self-affirmations.

Additional research investigated the link between acute and chronic stress and its impact on problem-solving abilities. This study included 80 people who said they had experienced chronic stress in the previous month. The participants were randomly assigned to one of two conditions: self-affirmation or control. Each participant completed 30 challenging problem-solving questions under a time constraint and in front of an evaluator. The results showed that the self-affirmed condition had better problem solving compared to the control condition. This research demonstrates that a self-affirmation practice can reduce everyday pressures and increase problem-solving performance.

What Are Your Executive Function Strengths and Weaknesses? Quiz

Executive function abilities are so important for executing activities involving problem-solving and thinking, so knowing your strengths and weaknesses may be beneficial. The quiz below can help you to identify areas where you may need help, as well as to allow you to better understand yourself, specifically how you learn and think.

Rate yourself on each of the skills listed below:

1 - Disagree, 2 - Somewhat Agree, 3 – Agree

Activation

1. My desk, backpack, and bedroom are free of clutter and are organized. ☐
2. I have the books or papers I need to complete my homework each night. ☐
3. I can keep track of deadlines. ☐
4. I write my homework in a planner. ☐
5. I can begin homework right away, even if it is not due until the next day. ☐
6. I always put things away properly. ☐
7. I can easily find things. ☐

Total Score: _____

Focus

1. I am not easily distracted. ☐
2. I focus on the task at hand. ☐
3. I have strategies to deal with distractions. ☐
4. I can concentrate to complete tasks. ☐
5. I do not daydream or zone out too frequently in school ☐
6. I am able to tune out unnecessary noises. ☐
7. I do not make careless mistakes. ☐

Total Score: _____

Effort

1. I can focus and concentrate on tasks, whether I am interested in them or not. ☐
2. I complete my work on time. ☐
3. I double-check my work. ☐
4. I do not let obstacles prevent me from finishing. ☐
5. I can complete long-term projects and assignments with no problem. ☐
6. I have enough time each night to get my work done. ☐
7. I work a reasonable amount of time on something before asking for help. ☐

Total Score: _____

Emotion

1. I am not get upset easily. ☐
2. My mood remains the same throughout the day. ☐
3. I never cry for no reason. ☐
4. I can disagree with family and friends and still like them. ☐
5. I can figure out what to do when faced with an obstacle. ☐
6. Getting a bad grade doesn't wreck my whole day. ☐
7. I use good coping strategies. ☐

Total Score: _____

176

Working Memory

1. I am able to remember what I need in order to complete tasks. ☐
2. I have adequate recall skills. ☐
3. I am able to keep a long list of things in mind. ☐
4. I usually remember important dates and information/facts. ☐
5. I have strategies to help me retain important information. ☐
6. I rarely need reminders. ☐
7. I can follow multi-step reminders. ☐
8. I can deal with information and not lose track of what I am doing. ☐

Total Score: _____

Action

1. I carefully consider the impact my actions have on others. ☐
2. I do not understand why people get upset with me ☐
3. I am not impulsive. ☐
4. I am not hyperactive. ☐
5. I can calm myself down after something exciting or upsetting happens. ☐
6. I can get back into the rhythm of school after a weekend or vacation. ☐

7. I do not have much trouble switching from one activity to another. ☐

Total Score: _____

Add up your points for each domain. High ratings indicate your strengths, while low scores are considered areas that need improvement.

Take a moment to think about the areas above that need improvement, and respond to the following questions:

1. Can you think of any examples in which you were impacted by an area where you need help?

_____

_____

_____

2. How did this negatively affect the situation? For example, did you lose something really important to you? Maybe you were late for class on the day you were doing something really fun and you missed out?

_____

_____

_____

3. In each of these situations, was there something you could

have done differently so it does not happen again?

_____

_____

_____

How Long Can You Stay on Task?

When you are doing your homework tonight, set a timer. As soon as you notice you stopped paying attention to the task, stop the timer. Record how long you were able to pay attention. Repeat this exercise ten times. At the end of the exercise, find your average time spent on task, or your average attention span.

Record your time here:

1._____

2._____

3._____

4._____

5. _____

6. _____

7. _____

8. _____

9. _____

10. _____

Now add the times together to get the total: _____

Divide by 10 to get your average attention span: _____

This number is an estimate of how long you can stay focused on a task. Focus for that length of time and then take a *quick* 2-3-minute break (stand, stretch, dance, get the wiggles out, etc.), and then repeat another block of work. You can work on gradually increasing your attention span by adding on one additional minute to each work block.

Improving Focus

It's good to have ways to keep yourself focused. Put a check next to the tools that you are already using that help you maintain focus. Circle the skills that you can try to practice.

__ Breathing skills

__ Self-talk

__ Reduce distractions

__ Quiet your mind

__ List and manage known distractions

__ Timers

__ Remove visual distractions

__ Phone apps

__ Tablet apps

__ Movement breaks

__ Daily planner

__ To-do list

__ Reminders

Pause Button Meditation

Throughout this workbook, we have been talking about the benefits of mindful meditation and taking a pause. In those moments, wouldn't it be nice to be able to hit a pause button, to freeze the moment and give us a little time to refocus? This pause button meditation helps us to imagine that possibility – and to visualize how helpful this could be in moments where we need it most.

- To start this meditation, get into a comfortable position, either sitting or lying down. Gently close your eyes, and start taking some slow dep, breaths.

- Create a picture in your mind of a button. You may make it whatever shape, size, or color you would like.

- When you press the button, you brain will take a little break. It will give you a moment to pause, slow down, cope with an emotion, or consider which action to take or response to give.

- Picture your pause button. What does your button need to look like to help you to remember to pause? Does it say the word "pause?" Does it say the word "stop?" Maybe it has a smiling face on its surface.

- Imagine a situation where you need to take this pause. Maybe you are in school and need to practice not speaking out of turn. Maybe you are with friends and have a big feeling. Can you picture this scenario? Over the next few breaths, create it in your mind.

183

- Now, imagine that pause button. On your next inhale, imagine pressing that pause button.
- Imagine that time is now frozen. Place your hands on your belly, and feel it get bigger with each inhale.
- Notice that right before you exhale, there is a small pause. Do you feel that moment of stillness? Do you feel your belly get smaller as you exhale? Do you feel that moment of pause before you inhale again?
- Press the pause button and take another slow inhale. Look for the pause in your breath at the top of your inhale, when your belly is its biggest. Notice the pause. Now slowly exhale, looking for the pause button when you are finished exhaling, you're your belly is its smallest. Press the pause button again and repeat for three big breaths!

Get Organized!

Use the job lists below to help you get organized and stay on task. Feel free to add more jobs or responsibilities that you have in your family.

MORNING JOBS	GETTING TO SCHOOL JOBS
Brush your teeth	Grab lunch
Get dressed	Get backpack
Brush your hair	Water bottle
Eat breakfast	Homework
	School supplies
	Gym clothes
	Library books

AFTER SCHOOL JOBS	BEDTIME JOBS
Have a snack	Take a bath
Do homework	Brush your teeth
Put homework away	Put on pajamas
Play	Set out clothes for tomorrow
Do chores	Put homework away

Working Memory Solutions

It takes practice to boost your memory. Fortunately, there are a few easy things you can do!

Below are six tricks that can help with memory. For each scenario below, list which memory trick would be most helpful.

- Place sticky notes in areas where you will see them as a visual reminder.
- Creating mnemonics (rhymes, songs, or acronyms) to help remember information.
- Make a to-do list to help organize all of your chores.
- Downloading apps to your phone that can help you stay organized, prioritized or remember what you have to do.
- Using self-talk to keep important information in mind, or to self-affirm that *you got this!*
- Take note of things you are likely to forget!

Scenarios:

1. You are in English class. Your teacher asks you to turn to page 42, read the first three paragraphs, and then answer questions 1 and 2. You open your book and start reading, but can't remember which questions you're supposed to answer. What can you do?

_____

_____

_____

2. In science class, you are getting ready to do an experiment. Your teacher is explaining what to do, but you have a question. Your teacher asks you to wait until she is finished, but you know you will forget! What can you do?

_____

_____

_____

3. Your parents ask you to stop at the convenience store and get milk, bread, eggs, and a snack! They ask you to *make sure you get everything!* What can you do to remember it all?

_____

_____

_____

4. You are hanging out and your best friend is talking about their weekend. You have something to share but want to wait until your friend is finished. What can you do?

_____

_____

_____

Applying Mindfulness to Daily Tasks

You can apply the idea of mindfulness to daily tasks as a great way to practice and improve your skills. Practice with the dishwashing meditation below but be sure to apply this skill to doing homework, doing chores, and sitting in class.

- As you turn the water on, pay attention to the sounds coming out of the tap. What does the temperature of the water feel like?
- Pick up a sponge, running your fingers over it. What does the texture feel like? Pay attention to the differences in the texture as the water hits it.
- Add some dish soap. What does it look like as it gets wet? How does it change? Can you see bubbles forming? When does it became fragrant? What does the soap feel like on your hands?
- As you start to wash the dishes notice how many differences textures or sensations do you feel? What are they?
- How does the sound of the water change when it is flowing from the faucet? When it lands on a dish? When the sponge runs through it? When you dip your hands in it?
- Are there any sounds coming off of the dish? When you scrub it? Perhaps scrapping food off?
- Continue mindfully washing dishes, keeping your thoughts anchored to this present moment.

Now that you have tried several practices and exercises aimed at improving executive function, take a moment to reflect on what you have tried, what has worked and what did not. Is there anything else you can try to help improve your executive function skills?

_____

_____

_____

_____

_____

Key Takeaways

Executive function difficulties look different in everyone, but in children with ADHD, they tend to appear in areas such as *activation, focus, effort, emotion, memory,* and *action.* This chapter provides tools to help parents and children in identifying their areas of strengths and weaknesses in regard to executive function, as well as practices and exercises to help improve areas of weakness.

Key Takeaways include:

- Using a timer to identify average attention span length.
- Skills check for improving focus
- A Pause Button Meditation to help stop, slow down, or cope with an emotion.
- A job list to help you stay on task.
- Scenarios to practice working through working memory difficulties.
- Applying mindfulness methods to daily tasks.

Chapter 10:
Creating Healthy Family Routines

Introduction

We all understand that rules and routines offer guidance and structure to our days. They are typically beneficial in creating healthy habits and can lead to positive mental health benefits such as a sense of safety and security, improved satisfaction, and productivity, as well as decreased levels of stress. With all of these benefits, it is not surprising that so much of the ADHD literature emphasizes putting routines in place. However, as we just discussed, the deficits common with executive function in children with ADHD makes creating and maintaining routines difficult.

I highlight this because it is important to remember that this is not *easy* for your child. They cannot simply *try harder*. The exercises below are designed to help both you and your child create routines that will support their executive function, as well as your mindfulness practices. Remember that there will be a dance between your wants and needs, as well as your child's wants, needs, and *capabilities.* You will need to be understanding, flexible, and patient as you and your child work *together* to identify goals, expectations, and routines that work.

Parents: You have come so far on your mindfulness journey. As you embark on this next leg, key components to keep in mind: your MAMAS goals, the strategies we discussed for both communicating and listening to your child, and offering validation and rewards.

Case Study

Boz is eight years old and has ADHD. Last year, Boz really struggled with hyperactivity. His teachers described him as angry, with a tendency to be violent. He often had tantrums at school, where he would throw himself on the floor kicking, screaming, and crying. When this would happen, he was sent to sit with the school counselor because the teachers could not calm him down. They knew that he had a hard time transitioning from one activity to another, but could not find a plan that worked for him. Whenever they gave him warnings that an activity was ending, Boz would immediately have an outburst.

His parents started working with a therapist, and together they put several steps in place to help Boz understand what comes next. Boz and his parents draw out a daily routine together on a white board using a fun blue marker that smells like blueberries. As part of the routine, Boz picks one chore from a list of three and one reward from a list of three, both of which will occur that day. Today, he will make sure his dirty clothes are in his hamper, and his reward is picking dessert that night. Boz is currently in his room, building Legos. To indicate to Boz that playtime is almost over, his parents start playing the song, *Life is a Highway*, from his favorite movie, *Cars*. Boz knows that when the song is over, so is playtime. He sees on his daily schedule that the next thing to do is wash his hands for dinner.

Affirmation

I am gentle with myself. I know I'm doing everything I can.

Parent

What are some of your non-negotiables as a parent? These are rules that you are not willing to compromise on because they are important to you for a variety of reasons, whether it is due to safety concerns, religious beliefs, health issues and more. *Examples may include: Always wearing a seatbelt; bedtime at 8pm, wearing a helmet when riding your bike.* Write your non-negotiables here:

_____

_____

_____

_____

Child

What are some things that you find really, really hard to do? Are there some things that you want your parent to know about? Write your answers here, or ask your parent to write them for you:

_____

_____

_____

_____

Let it Go!

I used to argue with my mother about the appropriate way to fold towels when I was younger. Our differing perspectives resulted in several disagreements, many of which ended in tears. This is an excellent example of something my mother could have let go of. Did it matter that the towels were folded differently if they were nicely folded?

A trigger for chaos and conflict in most homes is the parent and child having different perspective on how to complete chores and tasks. Both parent and child may *negotiable preferences* - things that they can be flexible or compromise on, such as doing homework before or after dinner, or having their chore be to set the table or dust the living room.

194

Parent: Below there is an image of two hands. On the *left* hand, list your non-negotiables. These are the rules that will be enforced. On the *right* hand, list your negotiable preferences, these are areas that you can *let* go and be open to compromise!

A Schedule for Chores and Tasks

Now that you both understand what is important, come up with a list of chores for your child that need to be completed. They can range from brushing your teeth to setting the table to walking the dog.

The parent can list the chores that need to be done (*consider both negotiables and non-negotiables, as well as child's feedback).*

1._____

2._____

3._____

4._____

5. _____

The child can then prioritize the order they happen:

1._____

2._____

3._____

4._____

5. _____

Make Chore Time Fun

Chore and household tasks do not need to be boring. Find ways to make them engaging and entertaining for the entire family. Some ideas including making it a game to see who can complete their chores the fastest (winner gets to pick the film for family movie night), playing upbeat music while you all work, and investing in some colorful cleaning tools. Start off by trying this once a week and then increase as you get more comfortable with this idea. As the novelty wears off, create incentives to keep it going, such as an extra 30 minutes of TV, or extra story time.

Daily Routine

Using a daily schedule can help the child with transitions and consistency, so that they can prepare for what comes next. *Do not forget to reward your child for tasks that are attempted or accomplished.*

Day:	**Time:**	**Task:**

Monthly Schedule

A monthly schedule is a helpful tool to visually remind you of upcoming appointments, events, dates and milestones. It serves many purposes as it can be as a tool for organization and memory prompting. I recommend using a paper calendar hung on the wall—at eye level with your child—so they can see what chores they are supposed to be completing. Fill out the calendar one month at a time, usually the last week of the previous month. Have your child cross off or X off the day when the chore is complete.

Sun	Mon	Tue	Wed	Thu	Fri	Sat

Improving Transitions

Transitioning between activities as well as waiting (such as in line or at a doctor's office) can be challenging, particularly for children with ADHD. We often are transitioning from a preferred activity to a less desirable one, which can be difficult if the child struggles with managing emotions. Additionally, waiting patiently or successfully transitioning to a new activity involves utilizing several aspects of executive function, such as activation and focus, which are common areas of difficulty for children with ADHD.

Parent: How hard is it to get your child to transition from one activity to the next? Does your child become impatient or act out when they have to wait (for example, in line or at the doctor's office)? In the space below, describe your child's behavior in these situations.

_____

_____

_____

Child: Does it feel hard to stop activity and move onto the next? Do you have a hard time waiting in line or at the doctor's office? Write about these events feel like for you below.

_____

_____

_____

How Can You Help Your Child Manage Transitions?

Transition strategies are techniques that support individuals in moving from one task to another. Below are six solutions that you can try over the next week to help your child transition or to help them in managing wait time better: Make sure to implement each strategy, one at a time, and seeing the effect it has on your child. Once you have an idea of what works, you can use multiple strategies together.

- Use a visual timer to indicate how long an activity or waiting period will last
- Build in extra time in the schedule if transitions are challenging
- Use a transition/waiting period toy: This is a special toy (or game for older children) that they can play with during these times
- Have a consistent way to signal that an activity time is over. This may be singing a song, playing a song or alarm on your phone, or doing a silly dance together.
- Give warnings: *Five more minutes until we have to leave for Grandma's! Three more minutes until we have to leave for Grandma's!*
- Set appropriate expectations and try to make it fun: *It looks like the post office line is long today. Let's play I Spy while we wait!*

Family Rituals

While establishing constant schedules and routines, make sure to also create family rituals that are consistent, but *fun* and highlight family values. Family rituals make everyone feel connected, provide a sense of identity and security, and can help build positive memories. Use your chore calendar to help keep track of your rituals.

Below are some popular family rituals. Take turns trying out each one every night, for a week, and see what works best for your family.

- Reading stories before bedtime
- Eating the same food every week, like Taco Tuesday
- Practicing gratitude
- Singing a good morning wake-up song together
- Leaving love notes in your child's lunchbox
- A special, secret handshake between child and parent
- Saturday morning breakfast ritual
- Share the highs and lows of your day at dinnertime

Mindfulness to Build Collaboration

Parent: Do you ever feel disappointment because your child did not complete their chores?

Child: Do you feel angry when your parent expects you to accomplish so much as a child?

Remember to employ mindfulness techniques to help you move through your negative emotions. Try mindfulness to bring you back to a state of calm, and then speak to each other about feelings. Use this opportunity to reassess negotiables and non-negotiables, as well as to incorporate input from each other into new objectives, expectations, and routines.

The following mindfulness practice can be done by parent and child, together, when feeling frustrated:

• Get into your comfortable position, eyes closed or relaxed, hands in your lap. Bring your attention to your breath. Stay here for a few moments, gradually slowing the breath, and focusing on the sensation of your lungs expanding and contracting. With each breath, think *I breathe in calm, I breathe out anger* (or frustration or disappointment).

• After a few moments, bring your attention to the physical sensation of this emotion in your body. Notice how your body is holding onto the negative emotion: do you feel tension in your neck and

202

shoulders? Jaw? Stomach? As you continue to breathe in calm, breathe out anger, allow each exhale to gently release those areas of tension.

- Bring your attention to your thoughts. What is fueling this negative emotion? Thoughts such as *it's not fair*, *I'm not putting up with this; This always happens;* etc. will continue to keep the negativity activated. As you breathe out anger, try to let it create a pause in the thoughts. The overplaying of the reasons why you are upset will only increase the emotions. Instead, continue to hold your awareness on your physical sensations of your breath and trying to relieve tension.

- As you move towards finishing this meditation, begin to prepare yourself for an open conversation about why you are upset. Bring to mind your active listening skills and recall the importance of using I-statements.

- Spend a few more moments taking deep inhales while thinking *I breathe in calm* and a slow, comforting exhale while thinking *I breathe out anger*.

Key Takeaways

Routines are important but can challenging to create and maintain for children with ADHD. This chapter offered exercises to help create routines that will support your child's executive function, as well as your mindfulness practices.

- Identify your parent non-negotiables and negotiable preferences.
- Using both non-negotiable and negotiable preferences, create a list of chores and tasks that need to be done. Let your child determine the order that they are completed.
- Create and display a daily routine and monthly calendar
- Help your child manage transitions or wait time, by using strategies such as utilizing a timer, providing verbal warnings, or managing expectations.
- Create family rituals
- Use mindfulness to help manage difficult emotions.

Chapter 11:
Building On What's Working

Introduction

This last chapter celebrates the work that you and your child have done so far, as well as all you have learned. Your mindfulness foundation has already been created, and hopefully you have begun to experience positive benefits.

We will now build on that foundation with a few final elements. The goal of this chapter is to use mindfulness practices to boost the child's self-esteem.

We want to use this positive momentum to build self-affirmations that can be used not only as mantras in meditations, but also as positive reminders of previous accomplishments, as well as a basis for gratitude.

Our focus also includes exercises to strengthen the relationship between parent and child. We do this specifically by curating prompts for dinnertime conversation and bringing awareness to the ways in which both we all feel loved by others. Lastly, we will talk about ways in which we can build on our mindfulness practice. The hope is that these last few exercises will help you and your child continue your mindfulness practice well into the future.

Case Study

Demi is 11 years old and has ADHD. Her symptoms are well managed by medication and bimonthly check-ins with her therapist, Dr. Ashe. Prior to working with Dr Ashe, Demi was problematic in the classroom. She was often out of her seat in class and would stand whenever she wanted to answer a question. Demi described being "too excited" to remain seated. Despite moving her seat to the front of the room, Demi would continually turn around and talk to whoever was sitting closest to her.

Now that Demi's behaviors are improved, her parents report to Dr Ashe that she seemed sad, commenting that she was aware of how different she was from her peers. Demi's grades were also poor, as she had missed a lot of instruction because of her behavior. Dr Ashe spoke with Demi and learned that her self-confidence was low as a consequence of the ADHD. Dr Ashe taught her to reframe the negative beliefs she had about herself, and to use self-affirmations to help stay positive and keep herself motivated.

During a math test, Demi reported to Dr Ashe that she felt bad because the test was hard. Looking around the room, Demi thought the other students knew how to solve the problems, but she "must be do dumb because I couldn't do it." Demi then remembered about reframing. She told herself, "It's OK if some of these problems are hard. There may be another one that I can answer." She also remembered her self-affirmation, *I can do anything I put my mind to.*" She also wrote this at the top of her math test so she wouldn't forget. This helped Demi keep her emotions in check and her mind on the test.

Affirmation

I can and will accomplish greatness.

Mindfulness, like any skill, takes practice. What is something you are good at that took a while to learn? Write about it in the space below.

_____

_____

_____

_____

Reframe Your Thinking

The goal here is to take your negative thoughts and reframe them into successful thoughts that can be motivating, as they help us believe in ourselves and all that we are capable of.

Instead of *I'm not good at this*, Think, *I need some practice.* Or, *I'm not good at this **yet**.*

Instead of *I don't know how*, Think, *I can learn how!*

What can you say to yourself instead of the following?
This is too hard for me.

I made a mistake. I'll never get it right.

I should just quit.

I'll never be good enough.

I never do anything right.

What if I get it wrong?

Dinnertime Conversation Starters

Mealtime conversations are a great way to improve communication, which is at the core of a healthy relationship. These talks can help strengthen family bonds, create more positive interactions, and provide an opportunity for positive connection. Practice using the following conversation starters:

- What is something that happened today that you are grateful for?
- If you could invite anyone to have dinner with us today, who would it be?
- What was the best part of your day?
- What are you most looking forward to tomorrow?
- If you could only eat one food for the rest of your life, what would it be?
- If you could stay up all night tonight, what would you do?
- What is something you can't live without?
- What is the craziest thing you have ever eaten?
- What was the hardest part of your day? How can we help?

Mindfulness Exercise for Self-Esteem

Mindfulness can be an additional tool for improving the way we feel about ourselves. In this practice, deep breathing is paired with self-affirmations that speaks to improving our self-value and self-worth. The affirmations included here can be substituted with any that resonate with you or your child.

- Get into a comfortable position, either sitting or lying down.
- Rest your hands gently in your lap, ensuring that your hands and fingers are relaxed and not holding tension.
- Softly close your eyes.
- Take a deep breath in and pause at the top of the inhale. Slowly breathe out.
- With each inhale imagine breathing in positivity. With each inhale, visualize the positivity spreading throughout your body.
- Imagine a warmth running through you as the positivity spreads
- As you breathe out, imagine exhaling negativity.
- Feel the warmth continuing to spread through you.

As you continue breathing and reflecting on the warmth, bring the following mantra to mind:

- *I am worthwhile.*
- *I am strong.*
- *I am capable.*

- *I am me.*
- *I am enough.*

I Feel Loved

What do you need to feel loved and accepted by others? Everyone's answer to this question is different and depends on a variety of things such as personality, life experiences, and expectations. Yet, knowing and understanding both what you and the important people in life need to feel loved can make a significant difference in your relationship. Having a better understanding of both ourselves and others can lead to better and stronger relationships with those we care about most.

Parent and child should each complete the survey below. Place a check next to each item that resonates with you. And then share what you learned.

I feel loved when:	Child	Parent
Someone compliments the way I look.		
Someone compliments the way I am dressed.		
Someone says something nice to me.		
Someone asks me how I am doing.		
Someone gives me a hug.		
Someone tells me they love me.		
Someone tells me they are proud of me.		

Someone says something nice or encouraging to me.		
Someone wants to spend time one-on-one with me.		
Someone sits and talks to me.		
Someone gives me a present.		
Someone gives me a card or letter.		
Someone surprises me in some way.		
Someone does something to help me.		
Someone tries to make my life easier.		
Someone helps me get my tasks (homework, chores, etc.) completed		

I Feel Loved Reflection

Take a look back at the items that you checked and answer the questions below.

1. What do you notice about the things that you need to feel loved? Are they similar or different?

_____

_____

2. Is there anyone in your life who does these things for you?

_____

_____

3. Based on this list, what can you tell someone about what you need to feel loved?

_____

_____

4. Parent: What did you learn about your child in this exercise? What can you do differently to help them feel loved? Tell your child.

_____

_____

5. Child: What did you learn about your parent in this exercise? What can you do differently to help them feel loved? Tell your parent

_____

_____

My Best Moments

      Taking a moment to reflect on our best moments can help us with self-appreciation, motivation, and gratitude. Additionally, we can use it as a reminder that despite obstacles, *we are capable*, *we are powerful*, and *we can do hard things*. Use this exercise to help remember your most joyful and best moments:

The kindest thing I have ever done was_____

The bravest thing I have ever done was_____

I am most proud of_____

The coolest thing I have ever done was_____

I was most confident when_____

I am most grateful for _____

My favorite memory is_____

The hardest thing I ever accomplished was_____

Notes to Self

- Practice saying the affirmations below to yourself every day, or using them in a mindfulness meditation. Based on the exercises you have completed so far in this chapter, are there any other self-affirmations you want to include? Write them in the space below.
- *I am enough*
- *I can get through anything*
- *I am powerful*
- *I am unique and special*
- *There is no one better than me*
- *I get better every day*

_____

_____

_____

_____

_____

We covered a lot of different exercises in this workbook. What exercise resonated with you there most? What about the exercise that you liked the least?

_____

_____

The Benefits of Yoga and Tai Chi

Research shows that exercise is especially beneficial for children with ADHD. There are several ways that being physically active can complement an ADHD treatment regimen. Participating in fitness activities forces individuals to rely on their working memory, and ability to focus and pay attention to either body movements or the game at hand. Additionally, exercise in general can contribute to improvements in alertness and mood.

Specifically, for children with ADHD, in addition to mindfulness, there are additional types of mind-body activities that can help with positive improvements in symptoms. Yoga, for example, has been found to have positive effects on mood, attention, and self-control. According to the Journal of Bodywork and Movement Therapies, practicing Tai Chi has been linked to decreases in anxiety, daydreaming, hyperactivity, and inappropriate emotions.

Other activities found to be especially beneficial for children with ADHD include biking, gymnastics, ballet, and most sports-related activities.

Key Takeaways

This chapter continued building mindfulness skills with additional exercises that can contribute to carrying your practice into the future. The specific goals of this chapter were to boost the child's self-esteem, build self-affirmations, strengthen the parent-child relationship, and continue to build a mindfulness practice that can be carried into the future. We:

- Reframed negative thoughts into their positive counterparts
- Used dinnertime conversation starters to help with the parent-child relationship
- Reflected on how we feel loved
- Recalled our best moments
- Practiced self-affirmations

Back Matter

A Final Note

I'm delighted that you made it to the end of this workbook! I hope your journey through mindfulness has been insightful and rewarding. You now possess a set of skills that can guide you in the years to come. Remember that this journey forward, like most things, will not be linear. There will be good days and bad days, easy days, and difficult ones. Through these peaks and valleys, your mindfulness skills can be your anchor, to help you navigate, process, reflect, and cope.

A few last reminders:

Keep a list of the mindfulness tools that you found comforting and helpful. In tough moments, it's not always easy to remember how to help ourselves.

Create a list of the wins! This is your successes and accomplishments both big and small. Use this list to help with your gratitude practice, as well as in times of positive reflection.

Keep your self-affirmations fresh. You, as well as your practice, are always evolving. Make sure your affirmations do, too. Change them as needed to remain motivated and empowered by their words.

Lastly, thank your child! Thank your child for being who they are and for the lessons they taught you. Thank them for teaching you so much about love, behavior, emotions, personality, and life. Thank them for starting a mindfulness practice with you. Despite the hard times, make sure you tell them you are grateful for them and that they are loved.

Best wishes on your mindfulness journey!

Resources

Additional resources to learn more about mindfulness for children:

—*A Handful of Quiet: Happiness in Four Pebbles* by *Thich Nhat Hanh*

—*Master of Mindfulness: How To Be Your Own Superhero in Times of Stress* by *Laurie Grossman*

—*Moody Cow Meditates* by *Kerry Lee Maclean*

—*Peaceful Piggy Meditation* by *Kerry Lee Maclean*

—*Sea Otter Cove: A Relaxation Story* by *Lori Lite*

—*I think, I am!* by *Louise Hay*

—*Unstoppable Me! 10 Ways to Soar Through Life* by *Wayne Dyer*

—*Mindfulness and Yoga Skills for Children and Adolescents* by *Barbara Neiman*

References

"About ADHD - Symptoms, Causes and Treatment." CHADD, June 13, 2019. https://chadd.org/about-adhd/overview/.

"Active Listening." Centers for Disease Control and Prevention. Centers for Disease Control and Prevention, November 5, 2019.

https://www.cdc.gov/parents/essentials/communication/activelisteni ng.html.

American Psychiatric Association. 2013. Diagnostic and Statistical Manual of Mental Disorders, 5th Edition. Washington, DC: American Psychiatric Association.

Assessment of Childhood Disorders, Fourth Edition. Chapter 2. Attention Deficit Hyperactivity Disorder. Edited by Mash, E.J. & Barkley, R.A. (2007)

Baumrind, Diana. "Effects of Authoritative Parental Control on Child Behavior." *Child Development* 37, no. 4 (1966): 887. https://doi.org/10.2307/1126611.

Boland, Heidi, Maura DiSalvo, Ronna Fried, K. Yvonne Woodworth, Timothy Wilens, Stephen V. Faraone, and Joseph Biederman. "A Literature Review and Meta-Analysis on the Effects of ADHD Medications on Functional Outcomes." *Journal of Psychiatric Research* 123 (2020): 21–30.

https://doi.org/10.1016/j.jpsychires.2020.01.006.

Condon, Paul, Gaëlle Desbordes, Willa B. Miller, and David DeSteno. "Meditation Increases Compassionate Responses to Suffering." *Psychological Science* 24, no. 10 (2013): 2125–27. https://doi.org/10.1177/0956797613485603.

Estes, Annette, Jeffrey Munson, Geraldine Dawson, Elizabeth Koehler, Xiao-Hua Zhou, and Robert Abbott. "Parenting Stress and Psychological Functioning among Mothers of Preschool Children with Autism and Developmental Delay." *Autism* 13, no. 4 (2009): 375–87. https://doi.org/10.1177/1362361309105658.

Fiorilli, Caterina, Teresa Grimaldi Capitello, Daniela Barni, Ilaria Buonomo, and Simonetta Gentile. "Predicting Adolescent Depression: The Interrelated Roles of Self-Esteem and Interpersonal Stressors." *Frontiers in Psychology* 10 (2019).

https://doi.org/10.3389/fpsyg.2019.00565.

"A Guide to Self-Care for Parents: Why Making Time for Yourself Matters." Waterford.org, April 24, 2020.

https://www.waterford.org/education/self-care-for-parents/.

Harpin, V A. "The Effect of ADHD on the Life of an Individual, Their Family, and Community from Preschool to Adult Life." *Archives of Disease in Childhood* 90, no. suppl_1 (2005): i2–i7. https://doi.org/10.1136/adc.2004.059006.

Hernandez-Reif, Maria, Field, Tiffany M., and Thimas, Eric. "Attention Deficit Hyperactivity Disorder: Benefits from Tai Chi." *Journal of Movement and Body Therapies 5,* no. 2 (2001): 120-123. https://doi.org/10.1054/jbmt.2000.0219

Hayakawa, Momoko, Alison Giovanelli, Michelle M. Englund, and Arthur J. Reynolds. "Not Just Academics: Paths of Longitudinal Effects from Parent Involvement to Substance Abuse in Emerging Adulthood." *Journal of Adolescent Health* 58, no. 4 (2016): 433–39. https://doi.org/10.1016/j.jadohealth.2015.11.007.

"Homeschool Printables from Preschool to Middle School!" Look! We're Learning! May 14, 2018.

https://www.lookwerelearning.com/homeschool-printables/.

Hölzel, Britta K., James Carmody, Mark Vangel, Christina Congleton, Sita M. Yerramsetti, Tim Gard, and Sara W. Lazar. "Mindfulness Practice Leads to Increases in Regional Brain Gray Matter Density." *Psychiatry Research: Neuroimaging* 191, no. 1 (2011): 36–43. https://doi.org/10.1016/j.pscychresns.2010.08.006.

Karelaia, Natalia, and Jochen Reb. "Improving Decision Making through Mindfulness." *Mindfulness in Organizations*, n.d., 163–89. https://doi.org/10.1017/cbo9781107587793.009.

KENDALL, JUDY. "Sibling Accounts of Attention Deficit Hyperactivity Disorder (ADHD)." *Family Process* 38, no. 1 (1999): 117–36. https://doi.org/10.1111/j.1545-5300.1999.00117.x.

Koudenburg, Namkje, Tom Postmes, and Ernestine H. Gordijn. "Disrupting the Flow: How Brief Silences in Group Conversations Affect Social Needs." *Journal of Experimental Social Psychology* 47, no. 2 (2011): 512–15.

https://doi.org/10.1016/j.jesp.2010.12.006.

Krick, Annika, and Jörg Felfe. "Who Benefits from Mindfulness? the Moderating Role of Personality and Social Norms for the Effectiveness on Psychological and Physiological Outcomes among Police Officers." *Journal of Occupational Health Psychology* 25, no. 2 (2020): 99–112.

https://doi.org/10.1037/ocp0000159.

Leavitt, Chelom E., Eva S. Lefkowitz, and Emily A. Waterman. "The Role of Sexual Mindfulness in Sexual Wellbeing, Relational Wellbeing, and Self-Esteem." *Journal of Sex & Marital Therapy* 45, no. 6 (2019): 497–509.

https://doi.org/10.1080/0092623x.2019.1572680.

Leitch, Sophie, Emma Sciberras, Brittany Post, Bibi Gerner, Nicole Rinehart, Jan M. Nicholson, and Subhadra Evans. "Experience of Stress in Parents of Children with ADHD: A Qualitative Study." *International Journal of Qualitative Studies on Health and Well-being* 14, no. 1 (2019): 1690091.

https://doi.org/10.1080/17482631.2019.1690091.

Levin, Elizabeth. "Baumrind's Parenting Styles." *Encyclopedia of Child Behavior and Development*, 2011, 213–15. https://doi.org/10.1007/978-0-387-79061-9_293.

Louis, Ashleigh. "Teach Your Kids the Value of Self-Care by Creating Healthy Habits." The Gottman Institute, February 10, 2021. https://www.gottman.com/blog/teach-kids-self-care-creating-healthy-habits/.

Markham, Laura, ed. Easy gratitude practices are a sure-fire way to replenish your joy. Accessed February 21, 2022. https://www.ahaparenting.com/read/how-to-change-your-happiness-set-point-with-gratitude.

Matthews, Gail. "Goals Research Summary." Boost Profits. Accessed April 18, 2022. https://www.boostprofits.com/wp-content/uploads/Goals-Research-Summary.pdf?x60870.

Minde, Klaus, Laurel Eakin, Lily Hechtman, Eric Ochs, Rachelle Bouffard, Brian Greenfield, and Karl Looper. "The Psychosocial Functioning of Children and Spouses of Adults with ADHD." *Journal of Child Psychology and Psychiatry* 44, no. 4 (2003): 637–46. https://doi.org/10.1111/1469-7610.00150.

Müller, Barbara C., Anastasija Gerasimova, and Simone M. Ritter. "Concentrative Meditation Influences Creativity by Increasing Cognitive Flexibility." *Psychology of Aesthetics, Creativity, and the Arts* 10, no. 3 (2016): 278–86. https://doi.org/10.1037/a0040335.

Nien, Jui-Ti, Chih-Han Wu, Kao-Teng Yang, Yu-Min Cho, Chien-Heng Chu, Yu-Kai Chang, and Chenglin Zhou. "Mindfulness Training Enhances Endurance Performance and Executive Functions in Athletes: An Event-Related Potential Study." *Neural Plasticity* 2020 (2020): 1–12.

https://doi.org/10.1155/2020/8213710.

"Parenting a Child with ADHD." CHADD, June 24, 2021. https://chadd.org/for-parents/overview/.

Parents, Start Here. "What Are Your Child's Strengths? This Is What You Need to Know." Start Here Parents! June 25, 2021. https://starthereparents.com/your-childs-strengths/.

Peterson, Tanya J. "How Your Parenting Style Can Affect Your Child's Mental Health." HealthyPlace. Accessed April 18, 2022. https://www.healthyplace.com/parenting/parenting-skills-strategies/how-your-parenting-style-can-affect-your-childs-mental-health.

Pozatek, Krissy. "Why It's Important to Set Healthy Boundaries with Your Kids." mindbodygreen. mindbodygreen, June 28, 2021. https://www.mindbodygreen.com/0-17051/why-its-important-to-set-healthy-boundaries-with-your-kids.html.

Redshaw, Rosalind, and Lynne McCormack. "'Being ADHD': A Qualitative Study." *Advances in Neurodevelopmental Disorders* 6, no. 1 (2022): 20–28. https://doi.org/10.1007/s41252-021-00227-5.

Sedgwick, Jane Ann, Andrew Merwood, and Philip Asherson. "The Positive Aspects of Attention Deficit Hyperactivity Disorder: A Qualitative Investigation of Successful Adults with ADHD." *ADHD Attention Deficit and Hyperactivity Disorders* 11, no. 3 (2018): 241–53. https://doi.org/10.1007/s12402-018-0277-6.

Tripp, Gail, Elizabeth A. Schaughency, Robyn Langlands, and Kelly Mouat. "Family Interactions in Children with and without ADHD." *Journal of Child and Family Studies* 16, no. 3 (2006): 385–400. https://doi.org/10.1007/s10826-006-9093-2.

Wymbs, Brian T., William E. Pelham, Brooke S. Molina, Elizabeth M. Gnagy, Tracey K. Wilson, and Joel B. Greenhouse. "Rate and Predictors of Divorce among Parents of Youths with ADHD." *Journal of Consulting and Clinical Psychology* 76, no. 5 (2008): 735–44. https://doi.org/10.1037/a0012719.

Zeidan, F., K. T. Martucci, R. A. Kraft, N. S. Gordon, J. G. McHaffie, and R. C. Coghill. "Brain Mechanisms Supporting the Modulation of Pain by Mindfulness Meditation." *Journal of Neuroscience* 31, no. 14 (2011): 5540–48.

https://doi.org/10.1523/jneurosci.5791-10.2011.

Zimmermann, Fernanda F., Beverley Burrell, and Jennifer Jordan. "The Acceptability and Potential Benefits of Mindfulness-Based Interventions in Improving Psychological Well-Being for Adults with Advanced Cancer: A Systematic Review." *Complementary Therapies in Clinical Practice* 30 (2018): 68–78. https://doi.org/10.1016/j.ctcp.2017.12.014.

About The Author

Nicole Andreoli, PhD is a clinical psychologist in New York City who works in private practice. Dr. Andreoli employs a cognitive behavioral approach and has worked with children, adolescents, and adults to address a variety of social, emotional, and behavioral disorders.

Dr. Andreoli has a strong foundation in the psychological and neuropsychological examination. She has performed psychological exams for people of all ages as well as for fitness for duty. Dr. Andreoli likes reading, traveling, exercising, meditating, and spending time with her husband and daughter when she is not working.

Milton Keynes UK
Ingram Content Group UK Ltd.
UKHW020614050923
428081UK00001B/7